Indian Economy

Visions, Reality, Challenges

Indian Economy

Visions, Reality, Challenges

Uma Narula

ATLANTIC
PUBLISHERS & DISTRIBUTORS (P) LTD

Published by

ATLANTIC

PUBLISHERS & DISTRIBUTORS (P) LTD

7/22, Ansari Road, Darya Ganj, New Delhi-110002
Phones : +91-11-40775252, 40775214, 23273880, 23275880
Fax : +91-11-23285873
Web : www.atlanticbooks.com
E-mail : orders@atlanticbooks.com

Branch Office: Chennai
Phones : +91-44-48531784, 28291383
E-mail : chennai@atlanticbooks.com

Printed & bound in India by Atlantic Print Services

Dedicated to

Visions & Reality of
Indian Economy
In Revolutionary Communication decades

For
My family and friends
Who
Envision this Reality

Preface

The book focuses on how achievement can occur if there is efficiency in economic management through instrumental economic reforms and liberalization, planning strategies for direction and pace for economy, remedies for structural and resource backwardness and functional welfare model for all. This requires involved efforts of the governance and people.

It is important how people and governance communicate their visions to each other. Our visions can be made successful by efforts of governance and people, economists and businesses.

The two techniques of Situational analysis and Scenario analysis provide an interesting background to the reader to assess the economic scenario conducive for economic development of people and governance.

These variables create configuration of change overtime according to the inputs of the economists, businesses, governance and people and also interaction of these variables in varied permutations. Communication plays significant role in how these inputs and interactions are created. Needless to mention, the present book will prove extremely useful to both the students as well as teachers of the concerned subject.

UMA NARULA

Contents

List of Figures

1

Introduction

The two configurations; Visions and Ideology, Performance and reality in social and economic contexts are significant for changing India and its people.

Indian mind set is transforming through socio-economic changes towards modernity and globalization. The cultural ways of Indians are changing fast since India is in the midst of social revolution—through economic reforms and communication revolutions worldwide. This human drama unfolds everyday and every step of our existence—sometimes very visible and sometimes subtle. Mindset is changing in multi-domains and multi-directions in the specific domains. People try to cope with the changing situations.

We, all in different age groups—old, middle, young and children do admit that we are different in many ways than what we were couple of decades back or years back. We admit that this change is necessary to keep pace with the changing times and changing contexts both in India and worldwide. We try to maintain the essence of *Indianness* and that essence is our *identity*. The identity (essence) is projected in our attitude, behavior, values, cultural practices; visions and performances in diverse domains. We redefine our identity through this process of change.

India has changed in the last five decades in multiple directions. It has moved forward, developed as well moved back in many domains and directions. This multidirectional movement has impacted Indian mindset both in positive and negative directions. The (people) Indians living in India and even those living in different parts of the world where they have migrated have undergone change and have impacted each other in many ways.

The multiple domains in which India has changed are, on one hand, economy, business, technology, computerization, telecommunication, education, public health, consumerism, leisure and entertainment, civil rights, family and social growth. On the other hand, the other domains and issues of governance and politics, terrorism-violence-war have changed India. The change in these multiple domains is in multi directions such as economic, political, social, cultural and religious. Changing India in these multiple domains has changed the Indian mindset and the change is tremendous. ***What is important is how the change both in positive and negative directions is coordinated between governance and people.***

Therefore, it will be of interest to assess how, why, when and to what extent they have changed. That is to suggest, in what way they have changed, the reasons for change, the process of change and the extent of change for development, modernity, globalization, aspirations and achievements. The 'Indian Image' worldwide is affected as the outcome of these changes. Thus it is important to assess the forms, the elements, contours and co-ordination of change in *Indianness* in multiple contexts.

Change has occurred in different coexisting generations of old, middle age, young and children in Indian society in these six decades. It has occurred among Indian people living in different geo areas of urban, urban slum, and rural. Even among the different socio-economic segments of society such as elite, middle class, low income, poor and shelter-less.

We do assume that Indian mindset has transformed through socio-economic change towards modernity and globalization to a greater extent. That there is impact of changed India and its governance on Indian mindset and vice versa. Moreover, how the change is coordinated between governance and people both in positive and negative directions also impact the mindset.

The basic Model of Modernity and Economic Visions of people and governance are the anchor points for assessment for *the changing Indian identity*. These anchor points are, most visible, visible and invisible overtime. The Economic Visions are interwoven in the multiple aspects of life. Events both at home and global happenings shape them.

> Urbanization ↔ Industrialization ↔ education ↔ employment ↔ exposure to media ↔ exposure to IT == opportunities, radical, globalization, innovation.

Fig.1.1. Basic Model of Modernity

The changing models over these six decades present insights about how Indians have changed vis-à-vis generations in different geo areas and in different socio-economic segments of the society.

The configurations of change pertaining to Indian mindset, that India can be the dominant player in multiple domains, the impact on India and its governance through such transformation of Indian mindset, and the forms, the elements, contours and coordination of change in Indian Identity in multiple contexts are interdependent and affect the significance and futility of such transformed roles in the global arena.

What hitches Indians will have to be the global dominant player?

India is emerging as a confident nation and is being recognized in several dimensions and is likely to be a dominant player in the international arena from various perspectives in the future. What motivates its people to aspire for being the dominant player in international and national contexts? How people strive to achieve it? Indians want to be entrepreneurs in multi domains, bold and risk taking. They are challengers as well as accept the challenges in the international markets. People are certainly confident of moving ahead despite the odds of not so stable, educated and forward looking polity, widespread corruption and bureaucratic hassles, low literacy, overpopulation and poverty.

Currently in 2000 decade, the key factors for Indians to be dominant players in businesses, industry and software development and applications are that they are challengers as well as accept the challenges in the international markets. They first challenged themselves by accepting the challenges in the domestic market and thence on they gained confidence to move on to international arenas.

They realized to set themselves in the above-mentioned areas; they must focus on technology, quality of products and services through high level of quality management, and be competitive in prices and in evolving and innovating continuously products and services. They found the opportunities to expand and challenge as India has the strength of tremendous manpower both skilled and unskilled. There is educated, talented and skilled manpower pool. Today, India has one time opportunity to make a 21st century miracle. They have battled against poor infrastructure and high cost of money at home.

They put the 'Made in India' brand for many products and services in the global marquee for many countries around the world by marketing itself abroad. How did it happen? This was mainly propelled by economic reforms of the 90s and driven by threats of extinction to find solutions to hurdles and to leverage India's advantage to emerge as a visible player in the supermarket. It exports in big numbers in garments, vehicles, cars and tractors, scooters, leather articles and shoes, software, packaged tea, steel, alkaline batteries, CDs and pharmaceuticals etc. Made by India is visible in many developing and developed countries around the world. The doctors in US and UK are prescribing medicines manufactured by Indian pharmaceutical companies like Ranbaxy, Dr. Reddy, Orchid, and Wockhard.

Indian Companies have shed non-core activities and brought in management changes and restructure themselves. They ramped up capacities to meet pent up demands. This was followed by reduction in import tariffs, lifting of quantitative restrictions that opened doors for competition. *Pricing is competitive, response is fast, and quality is best.*

Transnationals entered the Indian economy with new products and Indian manufacturers improved on designs and productivity. The cost efficiency, quality service levels give them a distinctive edge in the world markets. They even hired expats to gain credibility in international markets.

The evolution is not totally private effort. Government has also leveled the playing field. It lowered manufacturing inflation, and foreign exchange inflows to cut down the prime lending bank rates. Government has invested in highways, railways, airports, ports and other related infrastructure, technology development and training programs and healthcare, education and poverty related solutions etc.

India is making progress, juxtaposed with lower costs, improved scale of operations, investments in technology, and in technical and skilled manpower required. The entrepreneurs are passionate as well they share the belief that India is winning the place in global markets and they feel proud about it. Moreover, intellectual capital and cost efficiency has put India on the global map.

But to be a real dominant player, people have to match the quality, organization, competition, straightforwardness and honesty in dealings with non-material aspects of social and cultural life, and in polity. They must practice these values first at the national level and thence on project the same in international dealings. Development of its people both in material and non-material aspects is a big challenge for being dominant player.

Participatory Development and Good Governance model (PDGG) should be the focus. The focus is on strengthening the partnership approach to participatory development and good governance. This has radical implication for world economy. The emphasis is on micro level action contexts, local resistance to change, community participation, and empowerment of people through participation.

Economic and political liberalism is necessary for PDGG model. It is necessary that there should be vital connection between open, democratic, and accountable political systems, individual rights, and effective and equitable operations of economic systems with substantial reduction of poverty. The PDGG model addresses the role of multinationals in developing socio-economic development; growing global disparities; and the importance of dialogue between government and civil society actors.

There are ethical forces such as corruption in political, corporate, individuals, and in Mafia syndrome which can affect the economy in India. Corruption is a complex phenomenon when it becomes system based. In India corruption has become system based and system blamed. It is not easy to eradicate it. But positively it does destroy the development of healthy economy.

In India corruption is rampant at all levels and in all segments of the society. Both the rich and the poor are corrupt in their own way and justify their actions. The political leaders, bureaucrats, and even the lower rungs of the governance share the bounties of corruption in their own justified way.

Corrupt practices whether at any level holds up much of the economic growth. Corruption is a severe problem not because the people do not truly want integrity in public life; rather corruption flourishes because conditions are ripe for it.

The government institutions that provide the essential regulatory for a healthy economy are either weak or missing altogether. Deficiencies in banking and financial regulation, corporate governance, tax collections, and judicial systems, auditing controls and in number of other areas if not managed properly erode behavior and people's confidence and encourage corruption.

Common persons are being corrupt because the essential goods and services are not accessible to them without paying bribery. They can ill afford to pay it because of inadequate earnings. At the same time they may use corrupt means to make extra money. It is a dilemma because either way they must be corrupt for day to day survival.

Politicians are being corrupt. They are different kind of breed today. Most of them are no longer dedicated to public welfare concerns. They squander the public money in their party politics, political power struggles, and hoarding of personal assets in cash and property while in power. They get into all kinds of financial scams which the media reports so vividly but it is of no consequence in the long run as effective action is not taken against them. This kind of corruption perpetuates more corruption and gives wrong signals to the public as they are bad role models. Imagine, if government spends all that public money on public itself; where will be the economy?

Businesses are corrupt. They complain that even when the economy is liberalized, nothing works without bribing at each and every step. They have to follow the corrupt system to be successful in business. Bribery actually fuels the growth of excessive and discretionary regulations rather than lubricating business activity. But whom do they have to blame when they pass on poor quality of product to the consumer, when they adulterate food products at the cost of consumers' health and death, and when they short weight the products?

The Mafia syndrome grows in corrupt environment. Groups of people indulge in extortion of money, kidnapping for ransom, other cheating and fraudulent activities etc. Low checks, low law and order enforcement, and political backing is responsible in many cases.

Corruption is a complex phenomenon when it becomes system based. In India corruption has become system based and system blamed. It is not easy to eradicate it. Positively it does destroy the development of healthy economy.

Anti-corruption strategies should strengthen social, business, and monetary institutions. Both government and people can bring integrity in public life. In addition to reforming the government, we must recognize the powerful influence of public scrutiny and participation. This is important because it shines light not only on those who are corrupt but also on those who are struggling to bring integrity to public life. *Therefore all strategies must begin with a commitment to build economies and societies that are open, transparent, and ultimately accountable.*

Substantial action plan is needed to uproot corruption that has pervaded all levels of administration in the country. The administration and the politician-criminal nexus have to be broken. There is danger that our sensibilities may die if steps are not taken immediately to curb corruption. We need to develop sensibilities of the people so as to create a movement against corruption. There are many laws and rules to punish the corrupt elements. But laws by themselves have not been effective in removing corruption. We need a mass movement.

2

Economic Visions: India

Economic visions of India are presented through situation analysis of present economy, scenario analysis of People's economic-development choices and accepting the challenge of economic reforms and liberalization.

SITUATION ANALYSIS

Situation analysis of present economy depicts the reality in Indian society, its strengths and weaknesses, and threats and opportunities.

Both internal and external key driving forces that affect economic choices and behavior, and economy management is reflected in the Situation Analysis. It analyzes what is happening, why it is happening, and what should be done to be economically efficient.

Situation analysis of current economic scenarios supports our few assumption points. One, that interactive force of market forces and ethical forces has impact on how economy is shaped. The second assumption is that the economic planning may be based on sound principles and theories, and ideology; but pragmatically it is not successful if it is mismanaged. In day to day life people, face numerous situations which affect the economy when mishandled.

Situation Analysis of the economic scenario gives us insights into current economic strengths and weaknesses of Indian society.

Strengths

- The vast number of manpower can be strength if they are handled efficiently.

- Indian businesses take initiatives for growth both nationally and internationally.
- Science and technology initiatives are developing for global markets, such as Satellites launching, computer software development, and medicines and development of high grade pharmaceutical products etc.
- Government does plan for development though it is ideological.
- The constraints to economy are controllable.

Weaknesses

- Political instability, corruption, and criminality in politics can be major weakness. India needs political cleansing to get rid of irresponsible and unprincipled politics playing with peoples' mandate. Political corruption, low respect for laws, rules and regulations give wrong role models to people.
- Economic instability, economic crisis, and recession can lead to low economic growth. Economic cleansing is needed for wholesome development of economy of the masses. Checking corruption at all levels, black economy, and economic offences and focusing on consistent economic policies can do this.
- Weak Welfare Model particularly total neglect of the Absolute poor in real terms. Majority of the people cannot afford basic minimum needs and services. The need is to redefine employment policies and monitoring them overtime. Low employment is created by unskilled manpower, skills not matching the job market demands, and lack of upgrading of skills to match the jobs. Further, either the manpower demand forecasts are unrealistic or if they happen to be realistic demand forecasts, they are ignored and not implemented. Manpower forecasts must be matched by developing educational courses, skills and training programs. Job opportunities need to be created particularly for rural areas and for absolute poor.

- Low work ethics is problematic for high employment rate, productivity and prosperity. It affects economic efficiency.
- Low grade infrastructure and bottlenecks of roads, airports, railways, bridges, transport, electricity, power, sanitation, safe drinking water, and telecommunication etc. can affect economic growth.
- Ineffective laws, rules and regulations affect self-discipline of the people and nurture corruption at all levels.
- Overpopulation and urbanization when not handled efficiently become problematic.
- Deficit financial budget leads to international debts, and lower economic growth.
- India has a low percentage of highly skilled people in science and technology.

Opportunities

External:

- Indian Satellite Capacity of Pay Load Satellite Vehicle-1 (PLSV-1) can commercially launch satellites in the orbit.
- Compete in the Nuclear power development with other nations.
- Global provider for Computer Software development.
- Outsourcing and offshoring through BPO and KPOs and collaborative business models with the global partners can help develop the economy.

Future

- Infrastructure improvement can boost trade, industrial growth, and foreign investment.
- Skilled manpower is asset to the nation. Higher skills lead to higher earning, more purchasing power, and better quality of life.
- Government will have higher revenue if taxes are not evaded, and black economy is under control. Higher

revenue can be spent on development projects and making life more affordable for people.

- Focus on creating opportunities for non-agro rural jobs, rural markets for customize and innovative products can check urban migration of rural people. And check ills of urbanization.
- Overpopulation can be a national economic asset if it is self-disciplined, skilled, and have higher work ethics. These create more productivity and prosperity and therefore higher economic growth for the nation.
- Economic choices will be socially relevant.

Threats

External

- Political uncertainty can threat economic growth both internally and externally. External investors will not be willing to invest in country's infrastructure, which is needed urgently. Thus international credibility and connectivity will suffer.
- India will be a poor and weak nation due to low economic growth. The economies of people will suffer and so do their quality of life.
- If Absolute poor are not handled properly and given a status; they will perpetuate poverty and will be a drain on the nation's economy. 36% of the population are Absolute poor.
- If social opportunities of health, education, and employment are created but not implemented as planned and financed; they can pose a big threat to the nation.

Future

- Periodic Monitoring and Evaluation of development projects related to health, education, and employment is essential for proper implementation. Further action plans must be refocused according to monitoring and evaluation.
- Globalization of businesses and development projects and upgrading of manpower skills in globalization

contexts can boost economy and quality of life for people.

RECOMMENDED STRATEGIES AND ACTION PLANS

Challenge of globalization

India should reset its economic priorities to make them people-oriented rather than commodity related. This alone will help country meet the challenges of globalization. The people related economic policies must particularly focus on those who are worst off in society. Though raising economic growth is important, the ultimate objective should be to expand the ability of the most of sections of the society to earn a decent living. This assumes more importance as only by providing for a certain economic security to the poorest of the poor could the country meet the challenges of the globalization. These days there is no way any economy can escape the rapid process of integrating with the world economy. Globalization is a vehicle for progress that we cannot ignore.

Challenge of economic reforms and liberalization

In 1991, the government introduced liberalization policies but there was lack of initiative towards a radical change in social policies including basic education, health and creating more skilled labor. This has deep negative implications on the prospectus of improving living conditions and even chances of success of the market reforms themselves. The premise is that social opportunities should be given to people to grow. Social opportunities may be provided but unless strategies are worked out to implement them and monitor them in the process little will be gained.

There are two sets of views on economic policy being advocated on global plane for poor countries. One view attributed to international financial institutions is that the economies of poor countries should follow orthodox fiscal and monetary policies of high interest rates, balanced budgets with reliance on markets, and integration of domestic economies with world markets and international prices. In alternative view, the markets and price policies have to be used as a part of a plan.

As capital markets and markets in goods and services become more international, economies must respond to pressures that are not under the control of nation state. New technologies assist this process, allowing for the integration of production processes and swifter exchange of information. The previous pattern of mass production and consumption cannot be sustained under these circumstances. International capital shifts must be seen as of fundamental importance.

Market forces alone cannot determine economic future. Each country determines and draws a road map for economic reforms that would be based on its own skills, resources, strengths and vulnerabilities. As we enter the new millennium, this is a challenge that the developing countries must to be prepared to meet. It has been amply demonstrated that centrally planned and controlled economies were not right models for success or efficiency. To expect developing countries to continually liberalize, at an extreme pace, even within a rule based regime, may result in opposite of what is desirable.

PEOPLE'S ECONOMIC-DEVELOPMENT CHOICES: SCENARIO-ANALYSIS

Scenario Analysis presents different economic scenarios in specific permutations of Political-Development-Economic dimensions. Each alternative scenario has both positive and negative dimensions. It is for people to choose—what they want to gain or loose. People make economic choices for their own benefits. It is comparative learning experience for people when they compare their 'development–economic' situations now and at different periods. We encourage people to take the current economic situations as the anchor points rather than the historic period points.

The objective is to map out government and people's political, economic, and development concerns at different time periods and under different political nexus for selected economic issues.

If people have options to choose particular kind of political set ups or these are imposed upon them; they will have both positive and negative economic-development permutations that are likely to go along with these nexus. We discuss the four likely nexus for scenario analysis: Democratic political-economic-development, Permanent Dictatorship political-economic-development, Transitory Dictatorship political-economic-development, Monarchy/colonial political-economic development.

Scenario-analysis is two step analyses. First it maps out what particular nexus entails, what are likely expectations of people and government, and what is the current scenario. The second step is applying scenario analysis to particular cases/ countries in different time periods for selected economic issues.

On comparison, we will find that economic and development scenarios currently and for over-time periods will differ in developed countries (e.g. USA), and in other developing countries (India, China, Pakistan etc.). Some of them may be in different or same political nexus; but they have different economic and social development concerns.

Democracy-Politico-economic-development Nexus

Democratic rule is for the people, by the people through their elected representatives and through parliamentary system of government. The people choose the political leaders and political party to rule. The well-being of people is the main concern. What is expected from democracy is that government and people are equal partners in governance. The elected government delivers goods and services in the interest of people. People are self-reliant and make efforts to develop themselves. There is cooperation and coordination between people and government. Public issues are debated, best course is chosen and then implemented. There is reasonable economic growth to ensure provision of basic minimum needs for all. There is political and economic stability. In developing countries, in democratic set ups, the government encourages IEC (information, education, communication) programs for people. IEC programs create awareness about different issues, provide information and knowledge about them, and motivate people to participate in their implementation.

In democracy, the expectations as well as efforts of both

government and the people are to provide basic minimum needs to all, to aim at effective implementation of laws, rules and regulations to foster equality for all and deliver social and timely justice for all. Corruption is neither practiced nor it is a way of life. When people respect laws and rules, when they are not corrupt; it is likely, they will not evade taxes, nor is black money generated. This results in economic growth, circulation of money, and increase in purchasing power parity (PPP); higher rate of employment, resulting in higher purchasing power parity (PPP) to procure basic minimum needs and thus likelihood of decrease in poverty rate; both government and people provide social insurance and safety nets. Ideally people can identify democracy with equality, economic and political stability. *Does such scenario will make people contented? Chances are such an economic scenario will lead to economic growth and stability.*

Authoritarian Politico-economic-development Nexus

In authoritarian political government, the authoritarian head of the government could be a Dictator, or Monarch. The head is the supreme decision-making authority for country issues and thus in running the government. It is advocated that the decisions are taken in the best of people's interest without the people being consulted about them, or the issues being debated in public. The authoritarian head has his selected council of ministers, they help him in governance. These ministers are not the elected representatives of people. People are expected to abide by the authoritarian decisions and rules. The rate and type of economic and social development will depend on the kind of authoritarian head and the authority he wields. But on the whole the authoritarian head has greater personal stakes and personal benefits over the public good.

Not many countries worldwide are having authoritarian governments. In the recent past some African countries were having authoritarian governments. (of Uganda Idi Amin, Saddam Hussein in Iraq and others) People tolerated them for a short time only. There were revolts that erupted internally and from external factors to improve life for people and economic development.

Transitory Authoritarian Politico-economic-development Nexus

Any form of government whether democratic, authoritarian, monarchy or colonial rule does undergo transitory phases of authoritarian politics and rule. This becomes imperative at times to have firm control over running the government, or getting certain public issues implemented in the interest of people. At that point, the governing head thinks the public is too fragmented to act in its interests; and there is authoritarian rule for a transitory period.

Colonial Rule Politico-economic-development Nexus

Many developing countries had gone through colonial rule since early 19s. The colonial rule was mainly set up in these countries through trade links such as in India and African countries, through indentured labor for plantations such as in many Caribbean islands, Mauritius etc.; and even through setting up convicts-colonies such as in Australia and New Zealand, Andaman and Nicobar islands. The British, Portuguese, and Spanish were the big colonizers. In their home countries, they had monarchy. Mainly, the economic interests and wealth had driven these countries to bring other countries under their colonial domination. In the early 50s to 60s, most of these countries gained independence and self-rule through their struggles for political independence. After gaining independence some of these countries have set up democratic governments and others have set up authoritarian governments.

The colonizers used economic resources of the colonies to develop their own economies. They gained in wealth. But the economies of the colonized countries did not develop; rather over a long period of time these economies got fragmented and distorted. Colonists did maintain political peace, rules and discipline in those countries, and checks on other factors to safeguard their (Colonizers') interests. They ensured that these factors would not obstruct their rule.

Initially, they (Colonizers') did not disrupt the social conditions, traditions and customs of the particular society. Therefore, there was no effort to develop or bring about any social structural changes. Later on, over a long period of colonial domination, social structural reforms from humanitarian angle like education, women's freedom (e.g. child marriages, Sati, Thagi were abolished in India), clean environment, and medical facilities etc. were provided. But they did not interfere with land reforms or bonded labor practices in rural India as that would have created administrative hassles and problems for them.

For maintaining political peace, initially, as it happened in India, they had to battle with small indigenous rulers/tribal leaders as in African countries, who resisted their rule. Other princely rulers (in India) who agreed to pay allegiance to British rule were allowed to rule independently their princely States. British felt these steps were necessary for maintaining political stability in India. Thus even in British colonial rule of 100 years in India, there were many small and big Princely States where monarchy ruled.

Thus the economic and social development were only developed to the extent where they were conducive to their rule, maintaining social and political peace in the country and in conformity with practicing some of the values of their own society.

Monarchy Politico-economic-development Nexus

From historical perspective, strangling bureaucracy and limits on free enterprise are not Indian at all, they are imports. In the original and authentic India, commerce was not regulated by any one, and the culture grew and flourished on the bounty of trade to and from all over the world. Nobody could vote and rulers monopolized foreign policy, otherwise pretty much it was a free market for all. All that changed only with the arrival of the East India Company, which did set about controlling commerce. After the middle of the last century, the British Raj took over bureaucratizing every aspect of life in totality. India's post-independence socialism then applied another layer of alien thought and justification for crimping India's natural style.

Scenario-analysis of the above-mentioned five nexus overtime highlights people's economic and development choices over a period of time.

3

Economic Visions: Configuration of Change

Every country has visions for their economic growth leading to prosperity, progress and overall growth and development. Economic growth is the basic foundation and key for overall development since it provides resources. Though social structures and characteristics of the people, political leadership are significant at national and local levels. These days equally important are the globalization factors of technology, trade, human resources and financial resources. ***It is important how people and governance communicate their visions to each other.***

Our visions start with ideology always; therefore our economic visions are also ideal and real as well. We have to start with ideal and fit that with reality with planning and policy. Ideology focuses on objectives — both short and long terms goals of overall development. Planning should focus on resources and policies to achieve these goals. Reality is achievement through implementation.

Our economic visions should be functional and they could be made successful. The ultimate success of the visions lies in improving quality of human life. Our visions can be made successful by efforts of governance and people, economists and businesses. The economist must plan targets and policies that are realty oriented and functional to implement. The governance should attune visions to national socio-economic realities and imperatives and challenges of globalization. Businesses would demand and plan business growth both national and international within the framework of economic targets and policies. People would aspire for affordable, comfortable and quality of life. There will be economic achievement and growth if businesses grow and quality of human life is improved.

Achievement can occur if there is efficiency in economic management through instrumental economic reforms and liberalization, planning strategies for direction and pace of economy, remedies for structural and resource backwardness and functional welfare model for all. This requires involved efforts of the governance and people.

These variables create configuration of change overtime according to the inputs of the economists, businesses, governance and people and also interaction of these variables in varied permutations. Communication plays significant role in how these inputs and interactions are created.

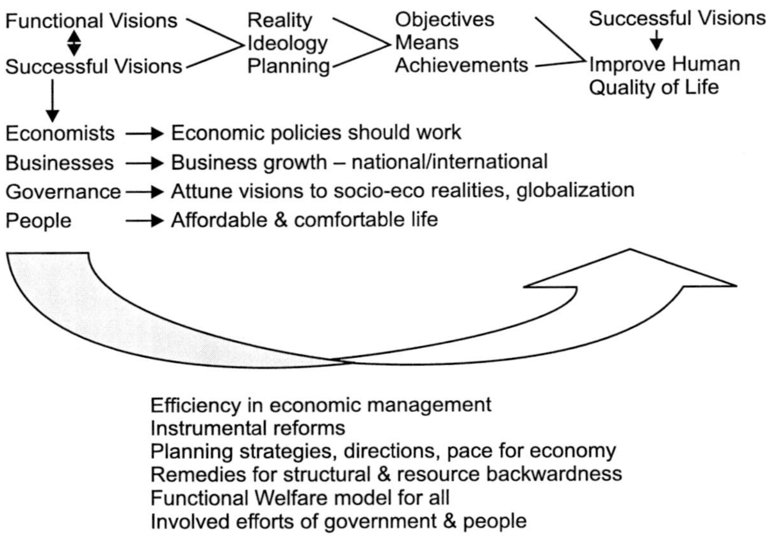

Fig. 3.1. Economic Visions: Configuration of Change

Economic visions are foundation of economic growth. In any developing country the two major focus for economic growth are: economic concerns of the society and country; and logic of economic development.

ECONOMIC CONCERNS

There are multiple economic concerns in a society and country. *First concern is, what kind of ideas, products and services a country produces and also has the capability to produce them.* a) Whether it can produce innovative ideas, products and services. There may be limitations of financial and human resources, if it is so, how it plans to overcome these hurdles by developing the capability of its people or by organizing international funds for developing the capability of the people and the facilities to operate such as labs, research and development facilities. Are people open to innovations; that is, it is progressive and open society to accept the challenges of innovations by experimenting these, adopting or rejecting innovations. The attitude to innovations matters more here than the financial limitations. b) Can it produce quality ideas, products and services which can compete nationally and internationally? and c) the technology level of indigenous, adopted, or borrowed technologies.

Second concern is how it is produced? In this context, the employee-management relations are important to develop the capability of human resources. Equally important are market forces and ethical forces, and efforts of people at local, national and international levels.

Market forces of globalizations, technology and economic liberalization have tremendously changed the business practices worldwide. Business practices have to keep pace with the rapid change in these forces to be successful. Best practices of yesterday may not serve the consumers of today; therefore the practices are on a continuum of change.

Ethical forces of corruption hampers economy. Corrupt practices whether at any level holds up much of the economic growth. Corruption can be political, in businesses and among common people. Corruption is a severe problem not because the people do not truly want integrity in public life. Rather corruption flourishes because conditions are ripe for it.

People need to be self reliant and participatory to identify issues and solutions; and to participate in implementations.

Third concern is how it is distributed. The logic of economic development is that there should be equitable development for all segments of the society; by eradicating and reducing poverty, and creating employment and providing basic minimum needs. Equitable development depends on the distribution of the output among people and growth productive capacity of all segments of the society. Such development should be sustainable. The economic players involved in this are the policy makers, governance, human and financial resources and people who need to make constant efforts to find alternative ways to handle quest for the best practices.

Communication messages, channels handle these concerns to create an equitable society.

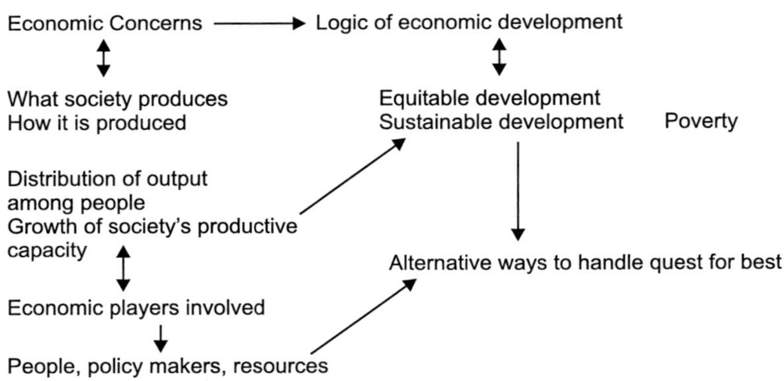

Fig. 3.2. Economic Concerns

ECONOMIC CHOICES

It is advocated that ***economic choice*** is a social process, and not the outcome of individual rational choices comparing cost and benefits of alternatives. Choices are not made in terms of relative utilities of a particular range of options, but are influenced by cultural expectations and preconceptions, by norms prevalent in society, and by own experience as well learning from the experiences of others. Expectations about the role of government, kinship obligations, and individual responsibility play a strong role in influencing views on economic choices in a welfare state. The common heuristics are important in understanding the limitations of human choices; such as the Anchor Points from which people start out when making a judgment.

The direction of choice cannot be simply assessed from options currently available. The influence of social context must be understood not only in terms of existing norms, but in how these norms operate overtime, and how they are reinforced, or contradicted by experience. Reference to Anchor points is important to understand assumptions that individuals have about their entitlements, obligations, and opportunities in a society.

ECONOMIC BEHAVIOR

Economic behavior cannot be understood as simply deliberative, rational, and instrumental. Cultural values, social context, and experiences influence how people choose. This suggests that economic choice is a social process and involves operation of the policies in concrete situations. People's beliefs, values, and attitudes relate to their actions as employers, workers, consumers, investors, and taxpayers.

Three factors are in particular importance in salience for economic choice and behavior—the shifts in circumstances of individual's life, wider economic and social changes, and ideological commitments at the political level.

The shifts in the circumstances of individual's life occur because of family, education, career, geographic opportunities and mobility effects his/her economic choices and behavior.

Changes in the styles of economic organizations, changes in the character of work in industrial, and information societies have political, social, and economic implications.

The social and political changes associated with a restructuring of economic activity lead to demands for a more open and flexible organization of patterns of work and provide the techniques that makes it possible. The ideological commitment at the political level is important for shaping the economic policies and choices. The political leaders set salient economic priorities for its people.

Public policy is built on the assumption that economic choice and behavior are motivated by rational choices and it argues that individuals in a market context will be rational actors in their own interests and that of their enterprises. Whereas, the empirical researches advocate that economic behavior in the context of markets and quasi-markets is strongly influenced by cultural factors. Ideas about obligations within the family, about equity, and about appropriate range of benefits that government should make available to the citizens contribute to the choices that people make. The significance of these factors varies in different policy areas, influenced by the relevance of different cultural assumptions and the strength with which they are held. Further, how these cultural assumptions interact with each other, with instrumental considerations, and with uncertain surrounding decisions affect economic behavior.

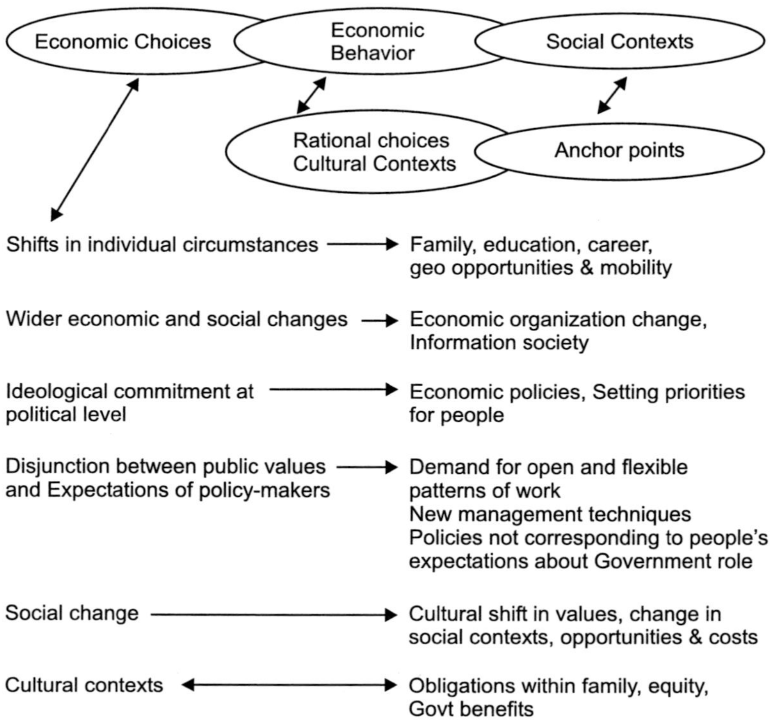

Fig. 3.3. Economic Choices and Behavior

SALIENT ECONOMIC ISSUES

The salient economic issues of employment, equality, and poverty are interdependent and interrelated issues. These pose challenges to economic development. The focus of welfare economics is to provide development oriented economic choices to its people by a nation, curbing poverty through anti-poverty policies. The economic policies are planned with a focus on equality, employment, social security and welfare of majority of the population. The challenge for welfare economics is how best to coordinate welfare spending for the citizens.

Economic inequalities may be inevitable in every society; its serious repercussions occur when the economic inequalities deprive people of basic necessities of life and the quality of life is low; when the gap between the have and have-nots is glaring enough to lead people to absolute poverty. At that point public policy interventions are needed to reduce these inequalities and their social outcomes.

Unemployment — underemployment, and non-participation in the labor market are pressing economic problems. Unemployment occurs when there are not enough opportunities for people for gainful work. This could be due to several reasons such as economic recessions, mismatching of jobs and job-skills demands etc.

Poverty — from the economic perspective poverty commonly implies lack of resources — money or material possessions that are necessary for individuals or households to consume goods and services above a certain subsistence level. Generally, the minimum level of goods and services that comprise the subsistence level is subjective. Although we agree that there has to be basic minimum needs for subsistence such as food with certain nutritional value, housing that meets some minimum standards, some level of health care, clothing, education, and such other basic goods and services. Yet there is no agreement as to what quantities and qualities of these items comprise the subsistence level of living. The particular subsistence level needs to be socially acceptable also.

Narula (2006) points that the blockages of socio-economic

benefits gap, knowledge-gap, and communication-gap removes the have-nots from the main stream society.

The efforts of governance are to create equitable society by handling salient economic issues efficiently. As we noted, the salient economic issues in any society are income equality, employment and poverty. Figure 3.4 given below highlights sub-issues pertaining to these main salient issues. Every society and democratic governance makes efforts to handle these to minimize the gaps among various segments of society.

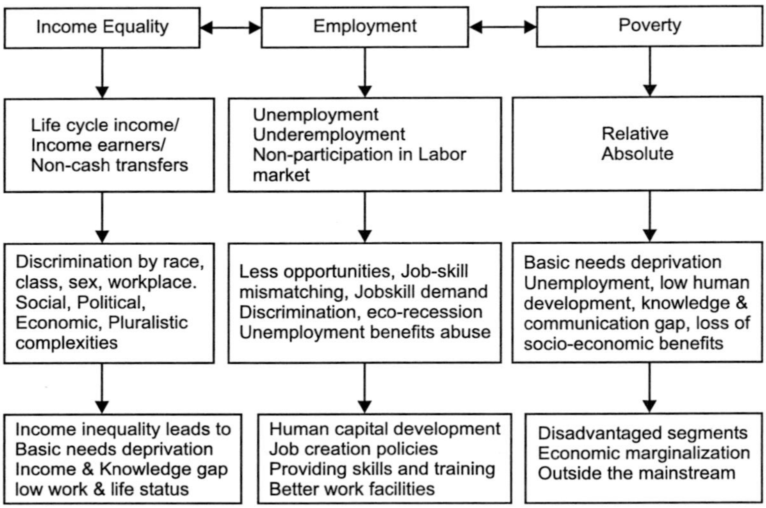

Fig. 3.4. Salient Economic Issues

Different regions of the world have different *welfare models* guided by their economic and social needs, and cultural norms. The core services of the welfare state are health, education, housing, and provisions for the old, ill, and unemployed. These are almost universally regarded as government responsibilities. Though the public agenda for welfare has not remained constant over the decades; it has changed with challenges of modernization.

Welfare Economics Models in both developed and developing countries present different issues and challenges.

The Welfare Economic Models tackle the issues and challenges of poverty and unemployment. In this context, European Model, American Model, Asian Model, and Indian Model present the diversity of issues and challenges. The challenges of Industrialism, Capitalism, and Modernization to Welfare State create a Functional Model of welfare. It is argued that societal development creates functional demand for social security and state intervention. Capitalist socio-economic relations and concomitant industrialization as the mode of production force State to meet requirements of stable social order.

Citizens understand that a scarcity of resources is a basic condition of life. Consequently public demands and expectations are tempered with realism. The public also understands that circumstances change. For example, the goals of full employment once thought essential for modern governments are not currently regarded realistic. Public also realizes that governments, whatever they may promise have limitations in what they can deliver. Modern public opinion is not necessarily disillusioned by the failures of politicians and governments. Public opinion recognizes that some political goals may be incompatible and that there is a trade-off between them.

The public mood does not slide into 'disillusionment' (as legitimacy theorists assume) since it cannot have everything and had to sacrifice for higher priority. Narula (1998) the disillusionment occurs as the government fails to deliver the basic minimum needs of the people. Narula & Pearce (1986) points that government's paternalistic attitude creates legitimacy crisis as government promises to deliver more but limited by its resources, it fails to do so and at the same time expect people to be self-reliant. Narula (1994 — 1999) points public opinion and the political system in India symbolize the complex strands of idealism and selfishness, commitment and dismay, planning and bureaucracy, blame and self-justification, and overwhelming discontent that comprise current Indian economic development.

The general public distinguishes between the limitations of democratic systems and particular parties or governments. The failings do not contaminate faith in governments. The

Legitimacy crisis theory fails to distinguish between the failure of politicians, of parties, of governments and the political system.

The General Economic Welfare Model given below in Figure 3.5 suggests that welfare models in general are designed to take care of economic and social needs and are guided by cultural norms of a society. It has welfare implications of the people as well need to develop human values, attitudes, behavior to fit modernity roles. The dimensions of economic welfare models are distributive justice, social welfare, human development, income growth, and purchasing power parities. These models are affected by improved benefits, demographic shifts, changed social attitudes, optimistic economic growth assumptions, increased life expectancy, and aging population. These models have to face the challenges of changing family structures, social exclusion, effects of relative poverty level, impact of globalizations and over and above limitations of government spending on welfare measures and schemes.

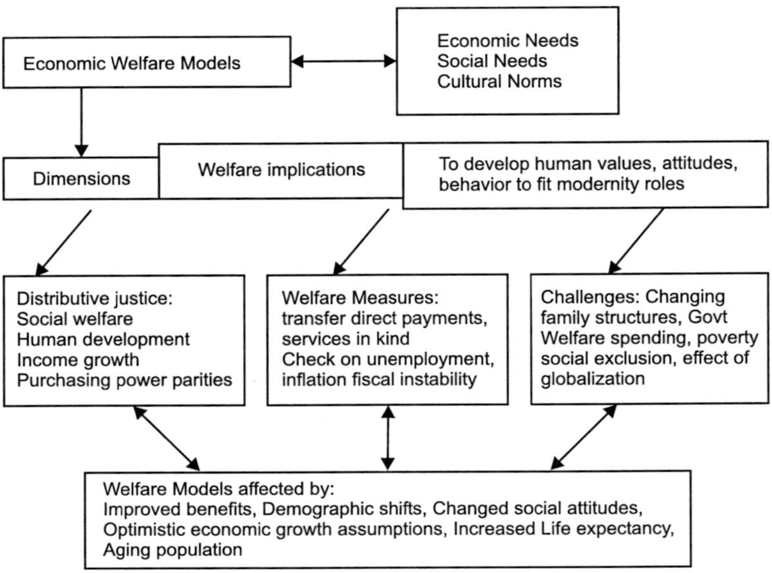

Fig. 3.5. General Economic Welfare Model

The social insurance for people in Indian economic welfare model is both cash and kind based. Urban and rural models are the two components of this economic welfare model. These differ because of the characteristics of these two segments of the society and the major focus of the livelihood in these segments. The rural economy is primarily agriculture based and small scale cottage industries are secondary. The urban economy is government and private sector driven in large scale industries, businesses, cottage industries, real estate and functioning of central, state and local governments through its various departments.

In India, the economic welfare model operates differently for two basic segments of society: Rural and Urban. Both of them focus on social insurance in cash and kind.

In urban model the social insurance in cash focus on pensions, provident fund, gratuity both for government and private organized sectors on retirement and death. It covers both the employee and family. Some of the pensions and provident plans are also partly contributory by the employees. But there is no structured social insurance plans for lower level self-employed, tertiary workers and absolute poor Social insurance in kind is given in free education, healthcare for all, subsidies for food and essentials, housing ownership loans for all government and private sector employees either by the employer or by banks and subsidized rental housing for government and private sector employees.

Though absolute poor are entitled to free education and health but due to social access factor they have almost negligible access to these facilities. They have no shelters and they live, suffer and die only on roadsides; winter or summer. They have no education, no skill, and have no employment. But they survive by begging and on charity. Even when leading this kind of life, they breed and add not only to the population but more and more to absolute poor category. The absolute poor are ignored in the mainstream society. They need more of social insurance focus.

In Rural Model, social insurance given in cash is nil for all. Though now they are encouraged to go for life insurance schemes, medical insurance schemes and public provident fund schemes. Since these schemes are self contributory, only those earning well may invest in these. Low earning or poor cannot benefit from these. But social insurance is provided to them in kind such as free education, healthcare and job-skill training for all. From time to time, employment guaranteed schemes are initiated for poor such as food for work and minimum employment guaranteed period of 100 days in a year in different government schemes from road building to other development schemes in the areas. This is accessible to both men and women. Agriculture subsidies are mostly provided by the government, and by some industrial groups under their social responsibility schemes.

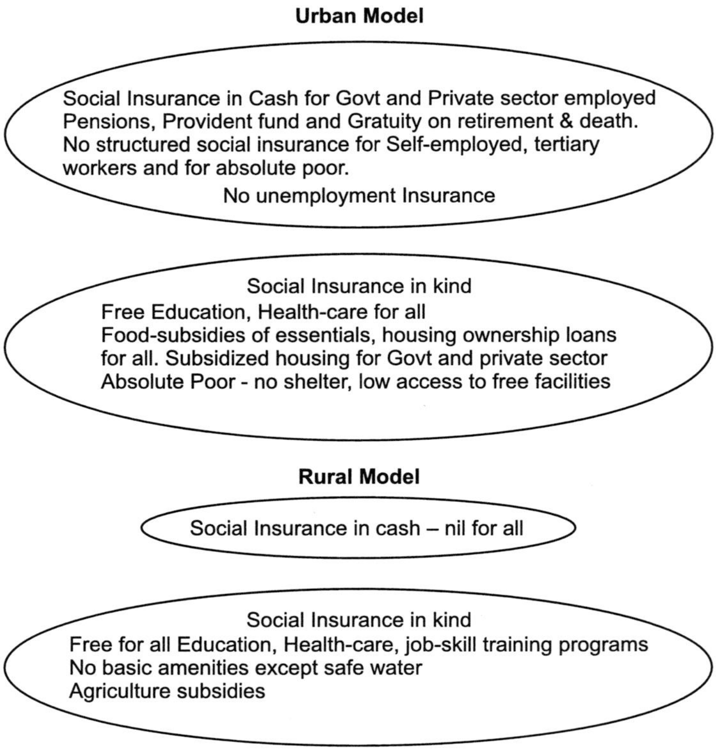

Fig. 3.6. Economic Welfare Model: India

PRAGMATICS OF INDIAN ECONOMY

The tenets of Indian economy are Democratic Socialism, Development Economic Planning, and Macroeconomics in general. A review of Indian planning for development since 50's (the first plan) through the five-year development plans to date — the 11th plan traces the development and planning dimensions. These are the planners' perception of the relationship between the national economics and community development. People have certain ideology of development based on their own values, aspirations, and expectations from planners and development functionaries for economic growth. Various plans focused on industrialization, agriculture revolution, people's participation models (Panchyat-Raj), and Basic Minimum needs and services (BMN, MNS), and poverty eradication programs. The focus of planning has been changing overtime due to internal and external economic exigencies.

Markets and economic policies must be integrated into a plan incorporating social priorities for development economic Planning. The Indian economy has achieved a measure of socially relevant economic plans including industrial and agriculture plans and prescription of policies for them.

It is argued that development economic planning policy in India will need a bifocal approach so long the problems of poverty and unemployment remain. The bifocal approach refers to a search for rules that aim at socially efficient use of resources, and also at the solution of the problem of structural backwardness.

Three factors are in particular importance in salience for economic choice and behavior—the shifts in circumstances of individual's life, wider economic and social changes, and ideological commitments at the political level. How these are applicable in the context of Indian economy is discussed.

The pragmatics of Indian economy are to deal with the issues of urbanization and overpopulation and to provide the masses with the basic minimum needs of food, safe drinking water, sanitation and other civic amenities, clothing, shelter education, employment, and purchasing power parity.

Economic stability, political stability and effective laws, rules and regulations and functional welfare models as social insurance are necessary to deal with these issues.

On the other hand, it wants to expand the businesses, its products and services in the context of technology and globalization to improve the economy culminating in better quality of life for its people.

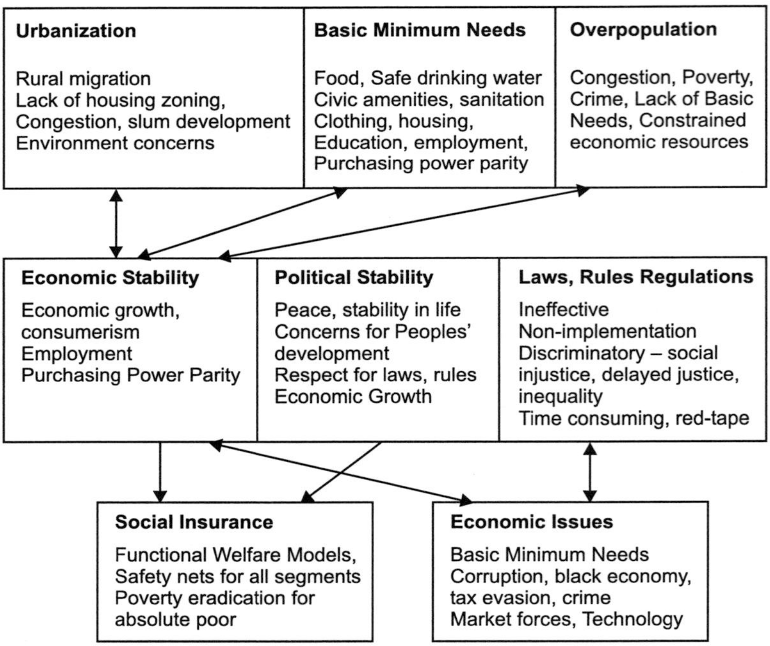

Fig. 3.7. Pragmatics of Indian Economy

The pragmatics of Indian society are impacted by both internal and external factors. The salient internal economic issues are basic minimum needs for people, overpopulation, urbanization, effective laws, corruption, black economy and tax evasion, government subsidies, price rise of commodities, crime, social insurance, employment, equality and poverty, and other diverse issues of privatization, market forces and technology, political stability. Further, it is salient how in turn these affect the economic growth and stability.

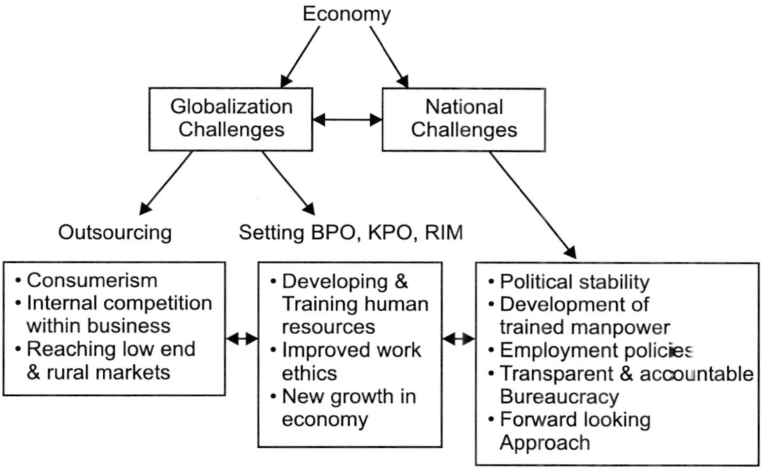

Fig. 3.8. Pragmatics of Indian Economy: Internal Factors

The external factors are foreign investment, international trade and competition, international aid and the challenges of globalization. Foreign investors are cautious about political stability and consistent economic policies of a country to invest in its markets. Over and above, they are much concerned about how the bureaucracy efficiently handles the clearing of plans and projects and rules and regulations for efficient investment and working in the country. This applies for both the foreign investors and their domestic counterpart/s with which they collaborate.

Moreover, a trained human resource with good work ethics and update technology can help meet the globalization challenges, higher productivity and competition, and higher employment in the country with affordable level of living. These factors can facilitate the visions of economic growth.

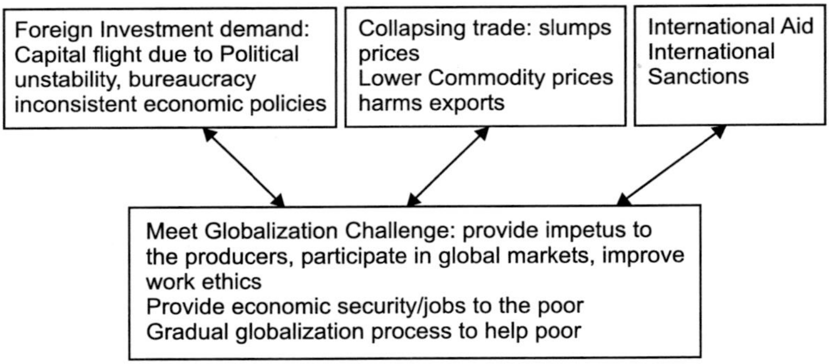

Fig. 3.9. Pragmatics of Indian Economy: External Factors

Governance and people both must meet challenges of economic reforms in India to fulfill the visions of economic prosperity of country and its people. These are created by both the internal and external factors of pragmatics of Indian economy as discussed in Figs. 3.8 & 3.9. If the governance wants economic growth and prosperity for its people; it must reform the way businesses are done both nationally and internationally, the consistent economic policies, policies conducive to the good of all segments of the society, spending resources for updating and developing technology and developing human resources and over and above the speed and efficiency of functioning in these areas.

CHALLENGES OF ECONOMIC REFORMS

There are six major challenges. *The main challenge is to provide economic and social opportunities to people by streamlining economic policies.* For this, it is important and necessary to develop and streamline skills and resources, develop opportunities and strengths of people and economy, and work out to improve on weaknesses, and threats and vulnerabilities of people and economy. These three challenges are interdependent. To achieve this, it will be necessary and imperative to make economies open, transparent and accountable. These three basic challenges call for the other three challenges of national efforts, citizens' efforts and international efforts.

National efforts will focus on political will to promote economic reforms and pro governance reforms to deliver the economic reforms efficiently through people oriented and socially relevant policies. *Citizens' efforts* to operate these reforms and achieve economic growth will depend on how they practice good work ethics of self-reliance, participation, efficiency, cooperation, responsibility and accountability and a forward looking approach to work and life both by the common people and civic society.

International capital shifts and investment in India, international aid for economic and infrastructure projects, and participation of India in global economy will enhance the economic activities and productivity, and targeted growth.

Thus *National efforts, Citizens' efforts and International efforts* combined together will facilitate in meeting the abovementioned six challenges and make these reforms a success.

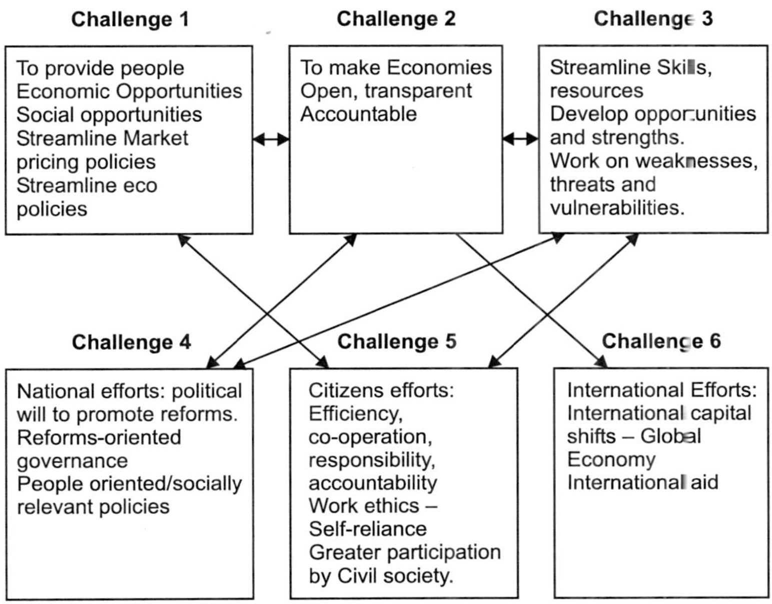

Fig. 3.10. Challenges: Economic Reforms in India

There are uphill tasks and targets in the above contexts of economic reforms in India. Infrastructure of roads, ports, airports, railways, bridges, flyovers, metro rails, airlines need to be modernized and expanded to match the increased economic activities in global contexts and giving these facilities world class standard. Basic telecommunication services must be developed in both urban and rural sectors to give better connectivity to people in all walks of life. Increased capacity and modes of power generation are required to give boost to economy both for industrialization, other businesses, and providing people infrastructure to lead quality of life. Developing economy of India does face the finance resource constrains for such modernization and expansion schemes but various project finance schemes both nationally and internationally are envisaged. Since economy and markets are open, funds and schemes are invited for investment and collaboration from any country partner with the requisite expertise. Thus first class expertise is planned. How they are planned, implemented and delivered through the combined efforts of people, governance and international agencies and institutions is imperative for fulfillment of its economic visions and its economic growth.

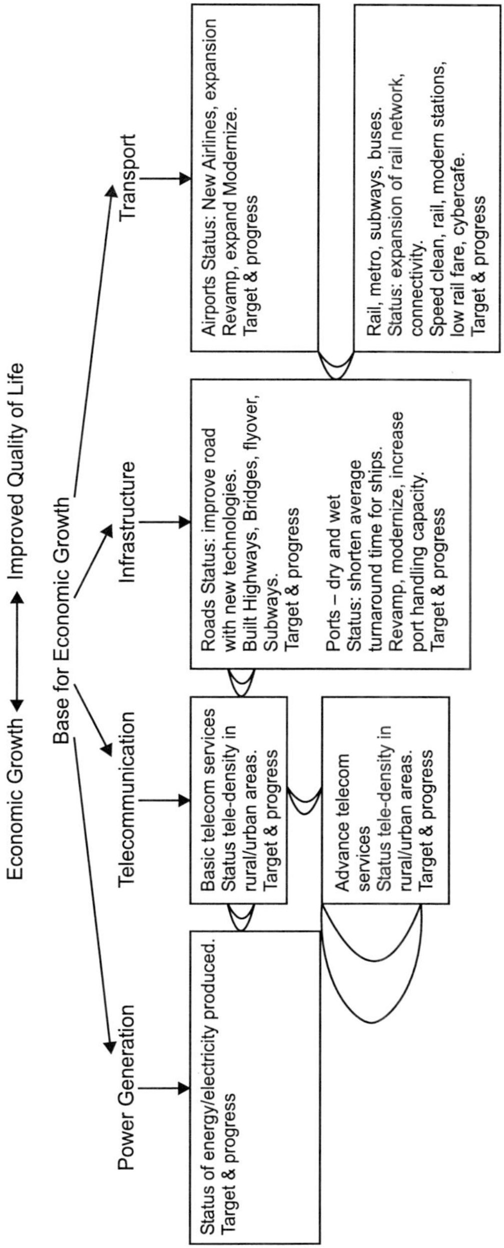

Fig. 3.11. Uphill Tasks: Targets and Progress

4

Technology Visions

In the present era technology advancement is imperative for economic growth. Both go together. Therefore, both economic and technology visions are necessary condition for economic growth. Technology visions presuppose information society context, information technology and promotion of technology. Innovation is base for technology development and promotion.

INNOVATIONS

Both social and material Innovations are necessary for economic growth. The dynamics of innovations are creativity, need and demand for novelty. The challenges posed are

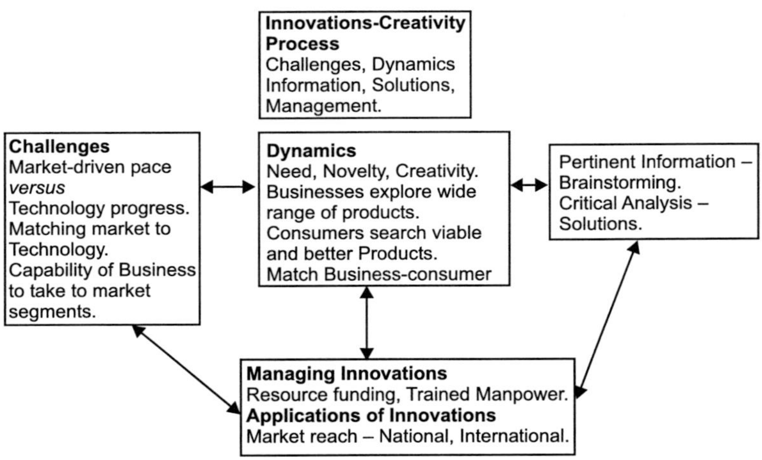

Fig. 4.1. Composite Model of Innovations

market-driven pace versus technology progress, matching market to technology and the capability of businesses to take to market segments. Equally important is managing innovations and its applications for economic growth through businesses in national and international markets. Resource funding and trained manpower are necessary for managing and applications of innovations.

Innovation is only worthwhile if it is focused on solving real-world problems. Anything else is just innovation for innovations' sake. The recent growth of digital content suggests how powerful innovation can be when harnessed to the real customer needs. The innovation is driven by customer as well by competition in technology. The system wide innovation aims at dramatically improving the end-user experience at every step. Technology born of innovation in addition to customer need has competitive advantage. The management in businesses must encourage and nurture innovations.

Even the efforts can be made to transform grassroots ideas into applications such as pedal activated washing machines, a device help to climb coconut trees for plucking coconut, or a potter who innovates mitticool terracotta fridge that doubles as water cooler filter and a Teflon coated terracotta tavva. These aim at conserving energy, managing without electricity and use of local material to multitask.

Poor has every right to improve their quality of life and not just aim at securing basic conveniences. We need to change the way we think about them. For instance, the government rural employment guarantee schemes, perceives rural people with only bodies and not minds. Hence its focus is on providing manual work like digging roads and stone breaking. The incredible India campaign on TV shows Rajasthan women carrying water pots on their heads. The image is perturbing. Why do women have to balance the heavy pots on their heads and go through the drudgery daily? There is a grassroots level innovative device to find a solution — a water jacket that could hold five liters in front and five at back. You have to fill it up, zip it and walk hands free. We throw away a match stick, use shorter sticks and provide each box with a stick holder or coat both ends of the stick with phosphorus (National Innovation Foundation, Deptt. of Science and Technology India).

The world is in the midst of sweeping transformation, from an industrial economy to creative economy that generates wealth by harnessing intellectual labor, intangible goods and human creative capabilities. Since 80s, this economy has generated the lion's share of new jobs, wages and salaries worldwide. India is well positioned to compete.

India also faces several challenges it ranks 41st of 45 countries on Kenney's Global Creativity Index. There are 3Ts of economic development. India does well on the first T, technology, ranking 23rd worldwide. It ranks 44th on the second T, talent and ranks 33 on third T, Tolerance, openness to self-expression, and to a wide range of social groups. India will have to be a magnet for talent from around the world in order to compete and win in the Creative age.

India's biggest challenge is that India's economic growth and innovations are concentrated on handful of regions. Virtually all significant technological innovations came from four city regions Banglore, Hyderabad, New Delhi, Pune. Outside these, other creative centers, large sections of India's population live hand to mouth existence. There is divide between creative haves and creative have-nots.

Still there is great tradition of creativity to build on. India has long valued the development of talent across multiple dimensions. Its internal diversity — religious, cultural, political and geographic, along with tolerance of dissent and openness to put aside influence and trade have provided this ecosystem with a constant influx of new ideas and people.

India needs to find ways to harness the full creative capability of its inhabitants across all industries, occupations, classes and geo regions. This would give India an advantage in the global creative economy and provide the world with a large-scale model for how development of human capabilities is the most effective route to true economic development.

India's future could depend on the strength of its 'creative economy'. India's future depends crucially on its ability to compete fully in the Creative Economy — not just in technology and software, but across design and entrepreneurship, arts, culture and entertainment; and the knowledge based professions of medicine, finance and law. While its creative assets outstrip those of China and other emerging competitors. India must address several challenges to increase its international competitiveness (Martin Kenney 2006).

Now that the industrial economy is giving way to creative economy, India should upgrade itself from high-value and high-impact innovations from quick-fix improvisations to tackle all problems. It is all about the growing power of ideas. Indians are getting amazingly creative in both technical and non-technical areas. There is phenomenal raw talent which has to be harnessed appropriately in the transition from local to global.

Indian businesses are fast realizing that the most intellectual property is the ideas contributed by its employees at whatever levels they may be and the grassroots innovators should be promoted and that is the new emerging spirit. The innovation process itself boosts economy.

Jack Welch said about companies in dynamic markets, 'when the rate of change outside exceeds the rate of change inside, the end is in sight.' Lots of companies over the globe see this. In a market place resonating with the sound of change, existing business models will run out of fuel. The booster can come over from innovations in business strategy. The core value of any knowledge-based company is innovation.

However innovations today have moved well beyond the scope of labs. Virtually every part of the company should be striving to innovate, to change, and to improve with the objective of achieving some new level of competitive advantage. The incremental improvement can tilt the scales in the market place. Some of the most successful companies of our times are those who have redefined themselves by using innovations.

India represents an age-old experiment in constant social innovations. Our education system should nurture the desire for innovations. This would give us the opportunity to ride the wave of innovations as we have done successfully with the global movements of outsourcing and offshoring.

The success of innovation is a function of the quality of the organization process for innovation rather than the amount of money spent. The spirit of innovation is being the best. In the quest for that we need a vision, pursued by disciplined managers, talented employees and nurturing environment.

In 2006, USA and India (during USA President George Bush visit) entered into important agreements which would boost Indian economy in global framework. One of them relates to innovation and knowledge economy. Emphasizing the importance of knowledge partnerships, it announced the establishment of a Bi-National science and technology commission which the US and the India will co-fund. It will generate collaborative partnerships in science and technology and promote industrial research and development. They agreed that USA and India would work together to promote innovation, creativity, and technological advancement by providing a vibrant intellectual property rights regime, and to cooperate in the field of intellectual property rights to include capacity building activities, human resource development and public awareness programs.

Indian Budget 2006 must stimulate investment, employment, rural regeneration and manufacturing. While it focuses on growth, it cannot forget that 40 million people are looking for jobs and another 20 million will join the labor force in the next five years by crossing the 18 years age mark. The budget must focus on employment elastic sectors of the Indian industry and address the vicious divide between urban and rural India. A second green revolution would bridge this gap. The key lies in stimulation of agribusiness, agro-processing and incentives for crop diversification. Cold chain technology, refrigeration, dehumidified warehouses, logistics and the entire value chain from farm to market must be given push.

No nation can be a superpower and the third largest economy in the world exists without a vibrant manufacturing sector.

Sixth Baramati Initiative (2006) centered on the theme of using ICTs in improving agriculture production and marketing. Earlier Montek Singh Ahluwalia, Deputy Chairman of Planning Commission has suggested that weaknesses in the extension system and credit delivery systems to the farmers must be addressed first for any kind of ICTs interventions to succeed.

For instance, ISRO devised a project where it used satellite to map the sea to find fish. While the information appears to be vital, the technology revolutionary, nobody accounted for the ability of the fish to swim. General wisdom suggests farmers are eagerly waiting for information about weather, prices and ways of improving productivity. Farmers are equally concerned about information on health care and loans.

INFORMATION SOCIETY CONTEXT

Information society presents a spirit of globalism with gradual disappearance of oral and traditional cultures and a quest for new cultural order, which goes beyond simple notion of information and communication. Information technologies create knowledge and sources of information. The ICT policies, infrastructure and the social system create information society. The information society produces information products and services; and professional technical personnel to facilitate these. Both these variables improve learning, education and skills in various sectors and improve employment. In a society, such information products and services transform businesses, society and political power which in turn contribute to economic development.

Development of information technologies in India has created an information society which is undergoing change as the policies, infrastructure and social systems are influenced by ongoing upgrading of these technologies whether computer, cell phones, television and radio, applications of Internet etc. These have improved learning, education and skills; and choice for entertainment and information. The information technologies are being used for development of business, social transformation and political power which in turn contribute to economic development.

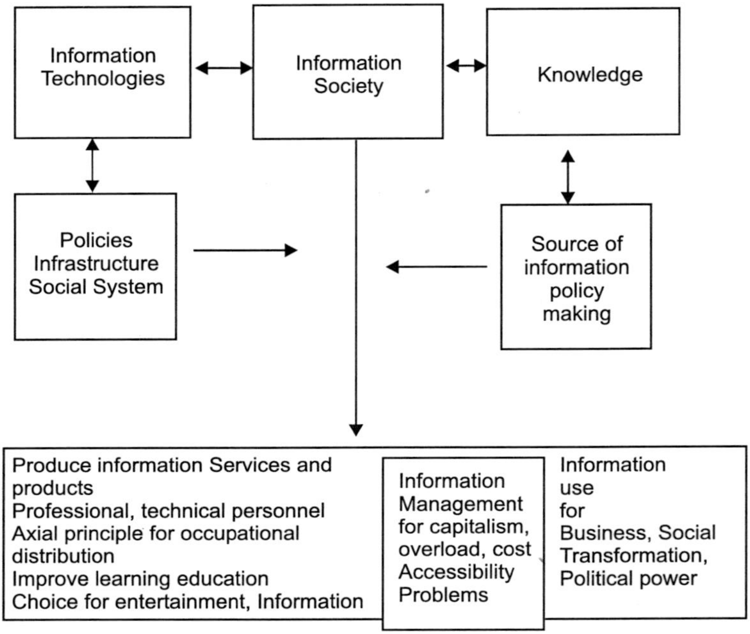

Fig. 4.2. Information Society: General Model

INFORMATION COMMUNICATION TECHNOLOGIES

Growing rate of Information technologies is impacting economic, social, cultural and technological visions. There is increased productivity leading to economic growth. It is transforming life styles of people and promoting a network society as well digital divide. The resulting globalization is creating international and intercultural communication, multiple identities as well fear and anxiety of losing cultural identity. This is true of India also. Not only it is upgrading its technologies for business, social transformation and entertainment but making it affordable for people to use. When the society is using advance Information technology in its varied applications; it focuses on varied dimensions to make information technology effective. Rapid technological change, unpredictability of consumer demands, and diversity of innovative applications create much uncertainty about the speed of development and diffusion; and economic, social, and cultural impact.

Social research can refine understanding of the complex roles that social, organizational and cultural processes play in the development of ICTs in various sectors of society. Yet the complexities and interdependencies of technological, organizational, and social change make prescriptions for policies and practice highly problematic and contingent on the special and historical context.

The social process of ICTs and its effect on the society represents a new perspective on social and behavioral processes. They seek guidance through research to improve social interventions using technology in domains such as education, mental health, work productivity etc. Scientists and technologists highlight the human side of electronic communications and they think about the social processes and effects of ICTs designs, applications and policies.

Communication technology visions present cultural challenges in every society. Such cultural challenges can facilitate or impede the economic visions and their achievement by the way they are handled by government, people, and media community. Therefore, for successful applications of technologies in various domains, it is important as well imperative to consider perspectives of government, people and media community.

In India, the government may have planned pro-social objectives of media channels in pluralistic society. It may encourage updated technologies for businesses and various management outputs by imports and exports and by development and research of indigenous technologies and by democratization of technologies. Government should be able to provide efficient, accessible, reliable and credible technologies. Social technology approach is necessary from people's perspective to assimilate the particular technology in their life style, to improve work ethics and skills, and for self-reliance and development. Media community perspective creates awareness, information, knowledge and motivation to diffuse innovative technologies in their life styles.

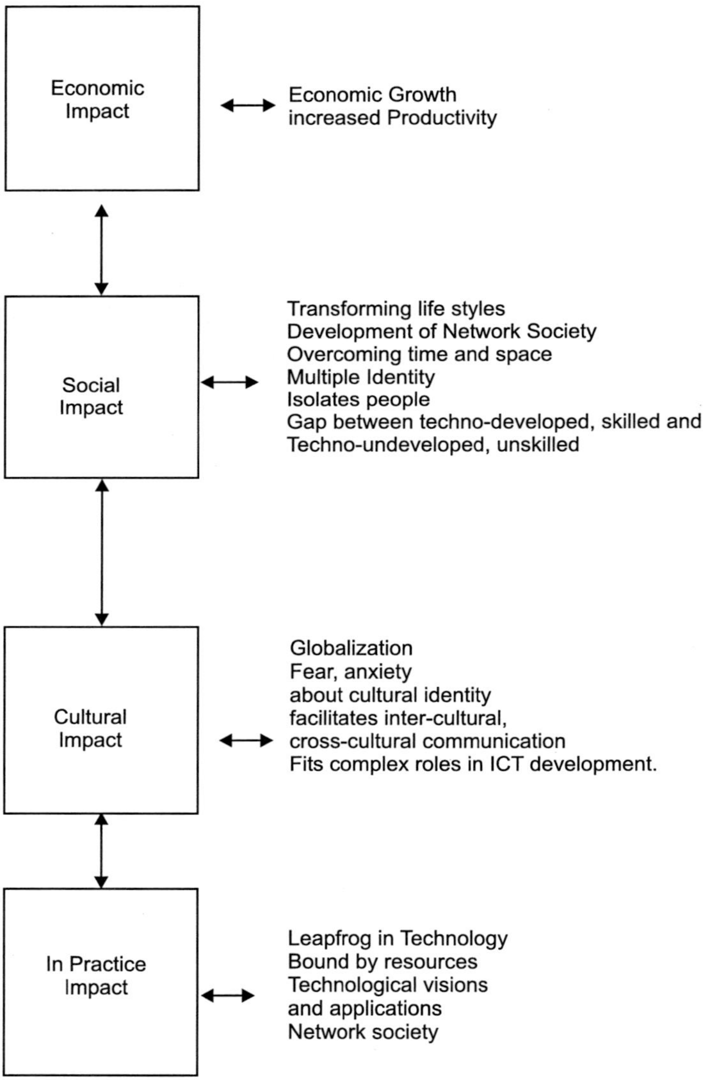

Fig. 4.3. Information Technology Impact

Social technologies are imperative for the diffusion of communication technologies. The concept of social technology is acceptance of a particular medium as well as the message meaning relayed through the individual and the social system. The performance demands of technology must fit into existing patterns of human interactions to be meaningful in the particular social system and must meet the standards of their social traditions that act as guideline for acceptance, rejection and censorship both by government and the people. The adoption of technology is a social decision so it has social implications.

The salient examples are computer and video technologies in India from 90s to date. In India, the adoption of computer was resisted in 90s. It had gone through the stages of anxiety, fear and apprehensions of losing jobs. In 2000 decades it is well accepted and ubiquitous. In 90s the video was accepted as an inexpensive means of entertainment through video parlors. Indian government has to censor the video entertainment for its misuse.

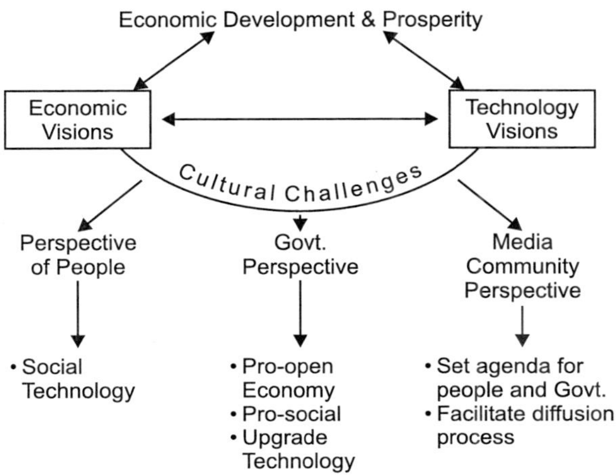

Fig. 4.4. Composite Model of Communication Technology

Every society differs in the race for information technology and building of information society. The model given in

Fig. 4.4 provides background to information technology efforts. The diffusion of technology at grassroots levels is aimed at social transformation and giving information power to people; through connectivity, accessibility and reliability of technologies.

In some countries, the advance technology model is accepted by national focus for historical, economic and ideological reasons by political will of the country. But the matching IT culture may not develop because of mismatched values and options. The mismatching technology options and bureaucratic decisions may also result in the adoption of low technology though the national focus may be for advance technology.

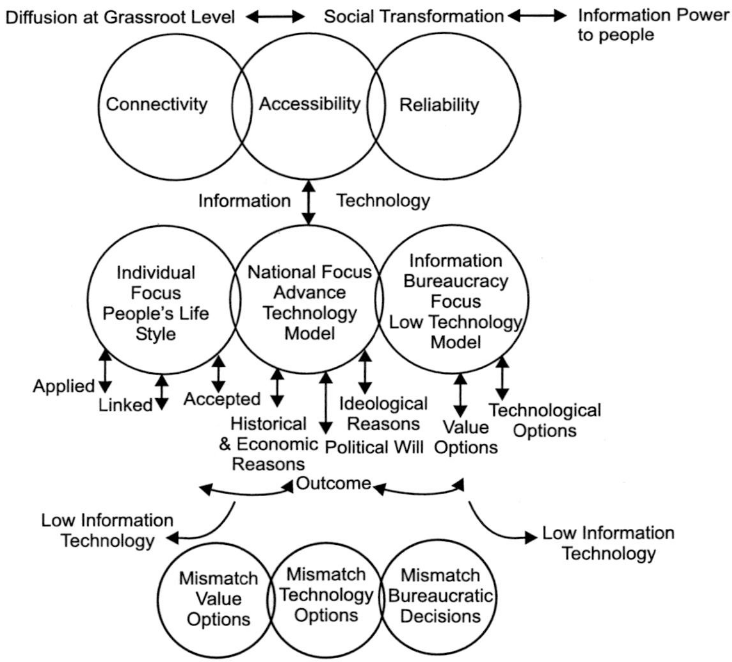

Fig. 4.5. Information Technology General Model

The advances in social, technology and communication national policies create information technology resources which create human resources through development of improved and higher level of skills, communication infrastructure and

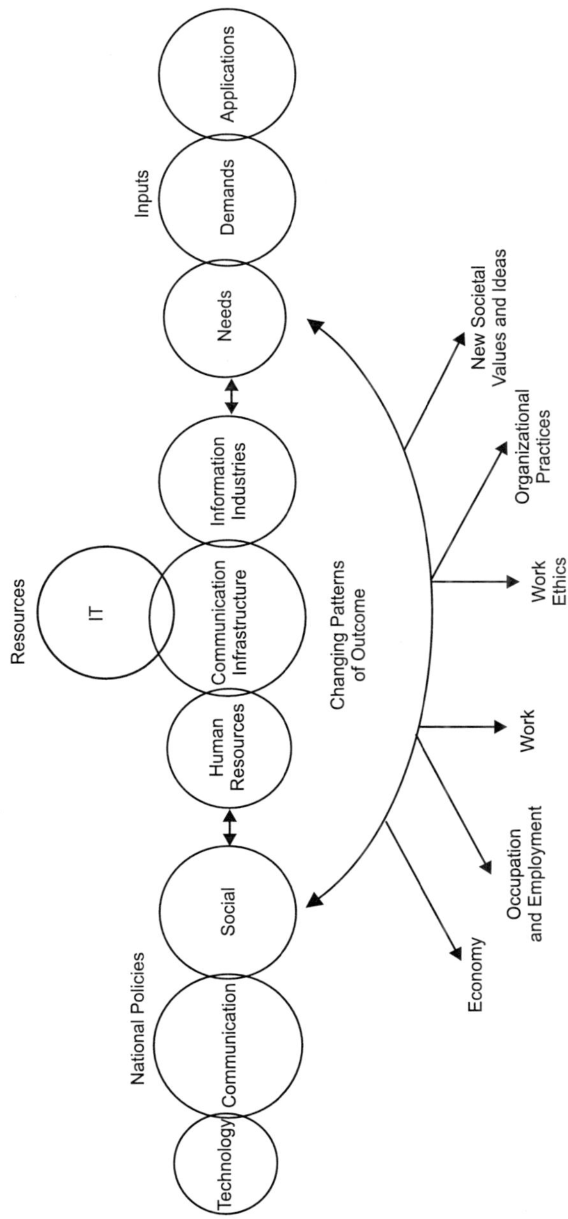

Fig. 4.6. Advance Information Technology Model

information industries. These depend on the needs and demands of people in various domains of life and how the applications of IT can facilitate these needs and demands. The advancement in IT change patterns of economy, through improved rate of employment, new occupations and new patterns of work, and improved work ethics and organizational practices. Over and above, the new social values and ideas result.

In 80s, the information technologies were resisted by people in India; though promoted by government at a low level because of resource and other pro-social constraints. In 90s, the political will was strong to overcome the people's resistance and it was accepted, linked and applied to people's life and work domains. India was focusing on Advance Information Technology Model through economic reforms and liberalization in late 90s and the advent of globalization. 2000 decades is witnessing the improved economic growth because of the advance information technology model which added the dimension of outsourcing and competition in various economic and business domains through developing IT expertise.

The economic visions of governance and political will in 80s, were enhanced by the economic visions of people and businesses of 90s but the economic visions of 2000 decades of people, businesses and governance through political will is leading to the fulfillment of those visions by economic development both in national and global framework and paving way for economic well being of the people, global economic, social and political leverage.

COMMUNICATIONS CONVERGENCE

India faces global challenge of connecting through communications convergence in current decades. It has been focusing and debating through a series of International conferences how to bring optimum connectivity to its people. In 2002, the theme 'Communication Convergence — the multi billion Indian opportunities' was successful in initiating new steps to bring the government and the corporate sector for promoting investments in Telecom and the related sectors. The second conference in Jan 2004 focused on the theme

'Communication Convergence — bridging the digital divide identified the challenges and opportunities for the Indian entrepreneur in taking the benefits of convergence to the people in India by phasing out the existing antiquated technology. The third conference held in Feb 2005 focused on the theme 'Communication Convergence — the change agent'. It identified the impact of convergence technology on the common citizen in a democratic society for better quality of life; at all the three levels of applications, enterprise and delivery.

The theme chosen for the fourth conference in 2006 is 'Communication convergence, connecting India the global challenge.' Access to Telecommunication services has become the prime mover of the socio-economic development in the information age. The role of telecommunications as an engine of growth with multiplier effect and social leveler has been well recognized globally. The governments the world over are making endeavors to bridge the prevailing information gap between the 'connected' and 'the not connected'. They are making efforts to ensure connectivity for universal access to basic telecommunication services at affordable prices. Governments of all countries have formulated their policies and regulatory guidelines with this end in view.

Rural India with its population of more than 700 million people has enormous potential in terms of economy and human resources. Recent experiments have highlighted that ICTs help to improve the timeliness and efficiency of rural farm operations and enhance income through producer-oriented markets. Further, village level knowledge centers disseminate essential knowledge to the rural population on health, family welfare, education, weather and disaster recovery etc. Therefore, knowledge connectivity does create multiple economic and social benefits to the people; and communication connectivity is a key component for harnessing the rural resources.

Urban India with its large low level middle class is also the 'not so connected'. They need communication convergence for improving their quality of life through upgrading personal and occupational skills for both social and economic benfits.

Nationwide connectivity with its conflicting requirements of availability, accessibility, and affordability poses challenges for Indian government, policy makers, leaders of industry and other stakeholders.

This conference would provide a platform to discuss and debate the various options for the choice of appropriate technology and effective implementation strategy to ensure meaningful connectivity to the 'not so connected' in a reasonable time frame. Such a strategy would go a long way in meeting the wider social and economic objectives of the nation.

5

Business Visions

GLOBALIZATION CONTEXTS

Challenges of globalization: These days there is no way any economy can escape the rapid process of integrating with the world economy. Globalization is a vehicle for progress that we cannot ignore. However what we have quickly learned from globalization trend is that the economic fate of a country is not solely in its own hands. In the globalized world, events in one corner of the world can have immense effect on the fortunes of others in far away corners and not at all involved with the events.

Global Communication is imperative these days to connect to people globally not only on just one on one basis but across many countries because of growing needs and demands on many fronts viz. political, economic, socio-cultural, technology etc. A network of communication across countries, inter-country and cross-country leads to globalization. Several countries communicate at bilateral or multilateral levels on specific issues.

The frequent inter-country and cross-country interactions depend on their (each country's) needs and demand to interact. These *Globalization contexts* could be economic including trade, political, technology, cultural, migration, social and tourism. The forces of interdependence of nations do create a close knit global economy and other systems. The force of globalization shifts power away from governments to private capital. ICTs have been the main driving force and facilitator in all these contexts.

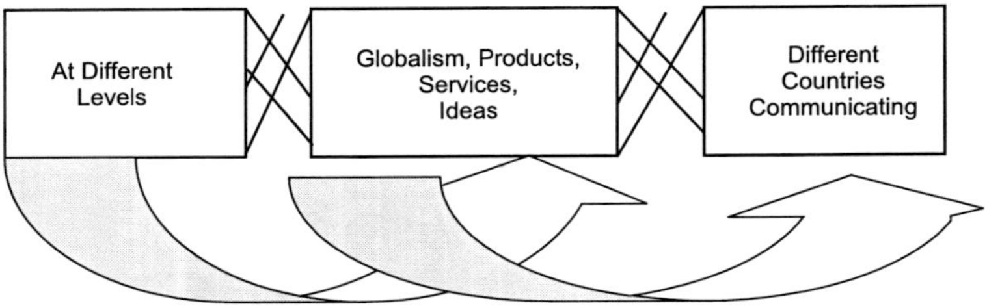

Fig. 5.1. Global Communication Model

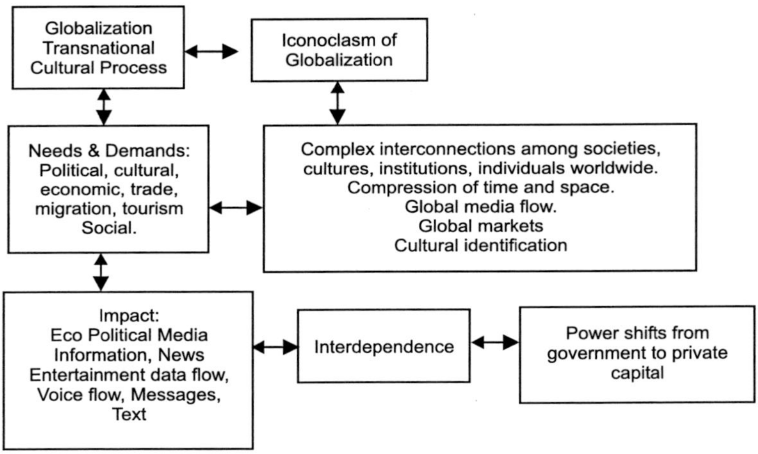

Fig. 5.2. Globalization Contexts

Economic context of globalization highlights that global communication industries study ways of customizing or innovating products suitable within geo-linguistic or geo-political regions. The local level producers are drawn on the global codes and conventions. The information and entertainment products champion predominantly the western ways of life, and values of capitalism and individualism. But there is exposure to different life styles of the world people. The enhanced and diversified trade and commerce markets usher countries into new economy. Unequal center and periphery relationships, hegemony versus rivalry, upper and lower class structures, and uneven cyclical developments affect world economy. The ideological categories and labels offer ideological self-satisfaction but impede and obscure the analysis of material real world, economic development, and real rather than ideal alternative choices it offers yesterday, today, and tomorrow.

There are three major trends that are shaping the future of the world. First, there is wide proliferation of the modern information and communication technologies. Second, there is increasing democratization of the social systems around the world. The third trend is the intensifying global expansion of mainly western-based corporations. Thus the convergence of these trends — communication technologies, political, and economic liberalization has transformed the way we live and communicate.

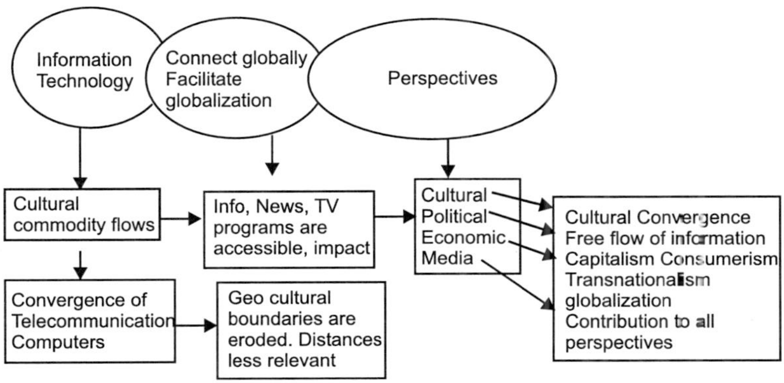

Fig. 5.3. Globalization of Technology

Interdependency Model addresses the issue of international interdependency for international development. Technological breakthroughs, innovations, re-inventions are researched and developed by many country's scientists and technologists. Ultimately the end product may be achieved and patented by one country but the ultimate objective is to let all benefit by it, whether it is telephone, electricity, television, radio, computer etc. The ICTs of present decade suggest global networking. Whether it is e-mail through computer, varied uses of telecommunications or broadcasting, and use of satellites. These ICTs work when there are global interconnected efforts for both hardware and software. These do not exist or survive by the efforts of a single country.

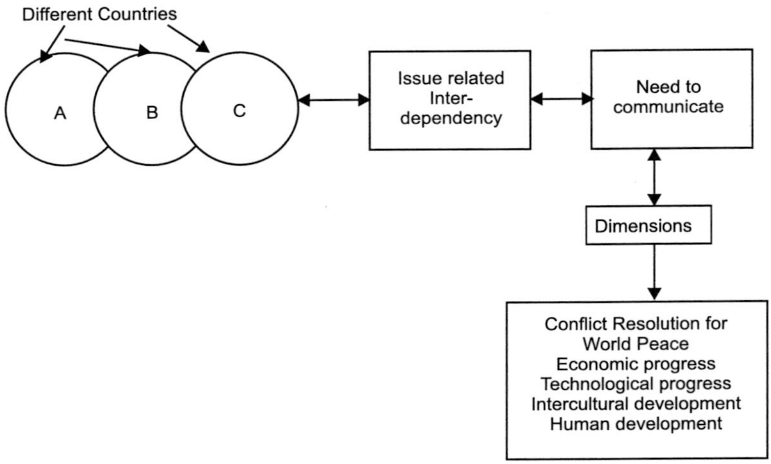

Fig. 5.4. Global Interdependency Model

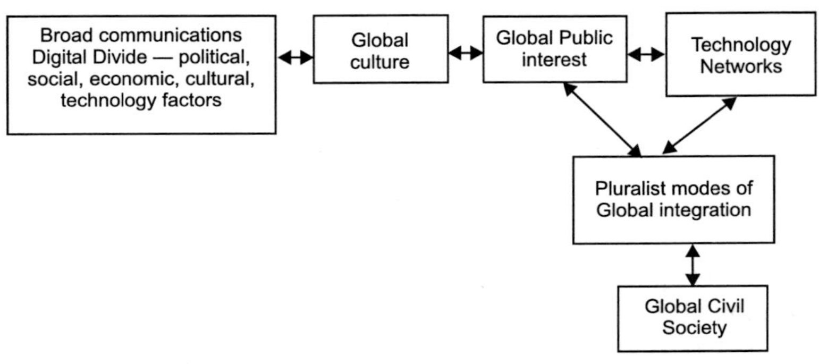

Fig. 5.5. Global Technology Networking Communication Model-1

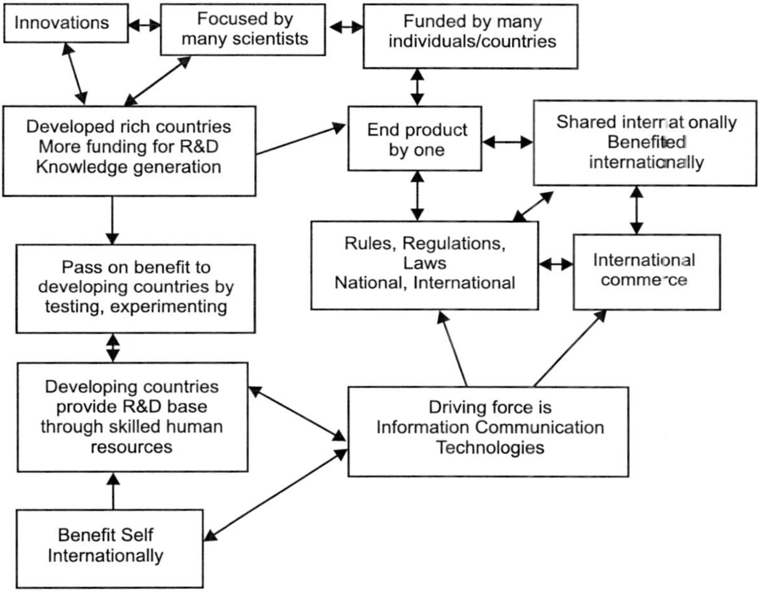

Fig. 5.6. Global Technology Networking Communication Model-2

Advancement in ICTs and technologies in general, its applications by people in their life and work and through global technology networking and interdependency contribute to economic development of people in societies at variable levels of development.

BUSINESS VISIONS

How we communicate our business visions through technology and developing human relationships and in global contexts does affect the economic growth.

Connectivity refers to the means by which people are connected to or are able to access communications channels such as the Internet, e-mail, computer and people networks. There are community initiatives that use the Internet and other digital communication networks and people networks to access markets, skills and opportunities to derive real economic benefits. Business communication framework focuses on perspectives, types of communication, contexts and patterns. It defines the scope, concepts and essential components of business communications and its tools. It presents the salient models of Business Communications.

Communication in any business operates from three perspectives: One, customer-supply chain relationships including both external and internal links; two, employee-management relationship including internal links only and customer-consumer-product relationships.

The dynamics of business communications are customer-supplier relationships in the context of product, services and people. Communications occurs in different forms in these relationships. It may be a set of data, information or knowledge about product, services and about people. These may be conveyed through technology, media, and oral interpersonal or through written word. The employee-management relationship is in the context of performance, productivity and human relations. These may be assessed and conveyed through technology, media, and oral interpersonal or through written word. But in addition, the human relations approach of developing reciprocal good attitude and behavior to create good and healthy work environments and professional development is important to assess and boost the performance and productivity in any business organization.

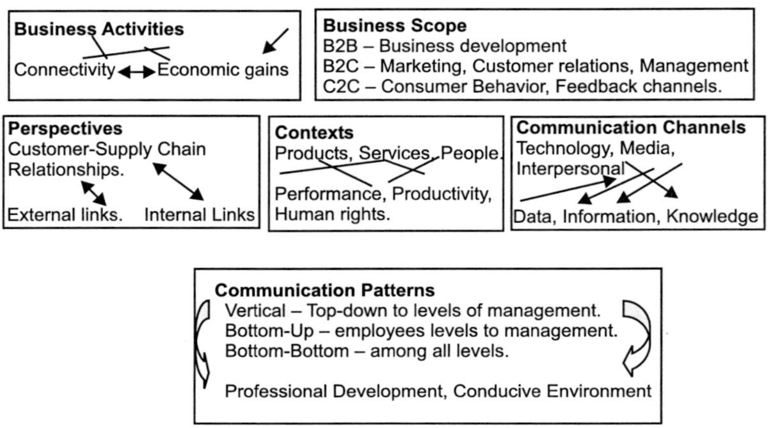

Fig. 5.7. Business Communication Framework

BUSINESS COMMUNICATION MODELS

We may understand the business concepts well but in practice it is important to manage the business reality well. Communication strategies are one of the components to manage business reality. The focus of business communication is on diverse dimensions of businesses. The various Business Communication Models take seven approaches. First is general approach to business communications. Second is special approach that handles business communications from various perspectives in specific aspects of different business sectors. Some of these may include negotiations in business dealings, marketing and management of products and services, product-cycle, advertisement and public relations, globalization and information technology. Third approach is communications for employee-management relationships in the context of development of business and professional development of people. It may be achieved through dialogue strategies among all levels in the organization, through training, coaching, mentoring and candid and frequent appraisals.

The fourth approach focuses on communications for human relations in businesses. These include employee relation management (ERM), customer relation management (CRM), product relation management (PRM) and resource management. Fifth approach focuses on business and economic intelligence and analysis, and economics of business communications. Sixth approach is the segmented market focus on the poor and those having low level purchasing capability. This presents Co-Creation Business Model. This is the recent new business model. So far the marketers have ignored this segment though in many developing countries they are almost 70% of the market. Seventh approach is the business communication to rural markets. This segment forms almost 70-80% of the market. Sixth and seventh approaches are unique to most of the developing countries. These seven approaches document seven business communication models. These models need different communication strategies to tap this market for economic development.

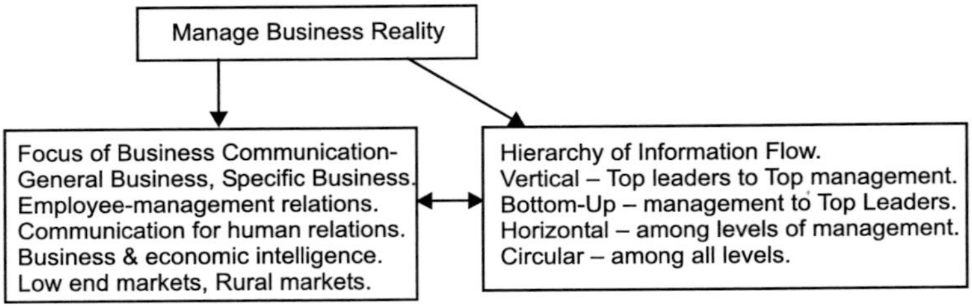

Fig. 5.8. Business Communication Model

BUSINESS MODEL

Every business organization will have business models according to its business objectives, products and services offered, business culture, and style of functioning of its top leaders. It may have one or multiple business models. As we have highlighted earlier, communication is the basic and essential component in all business models since all functions must be communicated in the right perspective for implementation of the business.

There are conventional and new business models. The conventional models have either already outdated or lost its utility and value because of changing business perspectives and market forces such as expansions of markets, emerging markets, and e-commerce, and knowledge economy etc. The advancement of technology both ICTs and business technologies have further created different businesses and therefore the need for varied business models and communication perspectives.

Over the years, business models have become much more sophisticated. Each of these business model innovations can give the company a sustainable competitive advantage. Companies must continuously rethink of their business designs and change their business models because of changing business environments and product values, consumers' profiles, and advancement in technologies. Ultimately the success or failure of a company depends first on how well its business designs and models match their customers' priorities and relationships with its external and internal links.

NEW BUSINESS MODELS

There are six salient new Business Models that have substantial impact on business, economy and marketing techniques. There is a paradigm shift with the advent of new models. These are, Business Intelligence Model, Co-Creation Business Model, Business Model for Rural Markets, Network Effect Business Model, Outsourcing and offshore Business Model, and Counterfeiting Business Model.

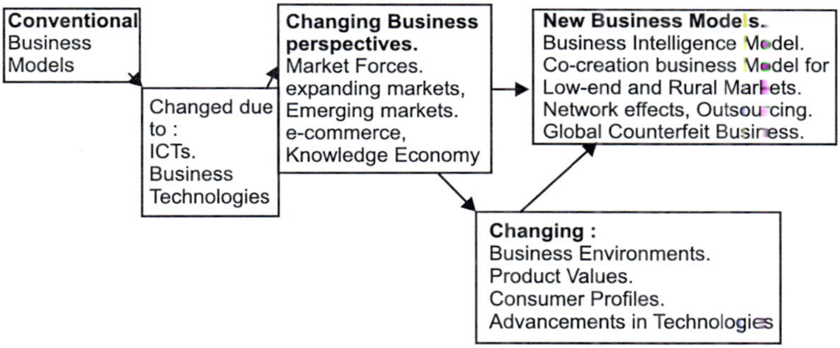

Fig. 5.9. New Business Models

Business Intelligence Model is in tune with changing dimensions and areas of businesses and the new and wider applications of ICTs. These create technological challenges such as technology management for cost effectiveness, competition and reaching new markets. The new market environments could be local, monopolistic to global.

HIGH-END AND LOW-END MARKETS

The Co-Creation Business Model is doing business with poor consumers with low purchasing capabilities. They are the masses but they do need the basics and necessities of life and can buy according to, 'as and when and as much' they can spend for their needs. It is a mass market. As such the poor consumers' major demand is 'sachet economy'. The main strategies of this business model are: tap this mass market, and do marketing of products according to their lifestyles without encouraging materialistic consumerism, produce according to their low purchasing power, mobility and accessibility. Thus there are three essential dimensions of Co-Creation Business Model:

(i) produce products and services for the poor and low income masses matching their purchasing power and capabilities,

(ii) enhance their purchasing power by providing micro-credit,

(iii) through micro-credit, businesses can also capture some share of market for regular products and services in course of time thus increasing their total market share.

Business Model for Rural Markets. In developing countries, 70-80% of their population lives in rural areas. They have low connectivity with inadequate physical infrastructures such as roads, public transport etc. They have low density of telephones and only some of them are exposed to electricity and TV etc. It is only recently that businesses understand the importance of rural markets; these have been ignored so far.

Rural Business Model is being developed now. This model focuses on five characteristics of rural markets and consumers:

(i) purchasing capability,

(ii) durable and non-durable consumer needs according to rural life styles. For example, they would need a different kind of food, different kind of soaps and detergents. Quite likely, there may not be any market for toilet tissue and paper napkins,

(iii) sachet economy will be the priority for durable consumer goods,

(iv) businesses need to tap the market for farm implements, accessories and farm goods and provide doorstep delivery system,

(v) delivery system is the most crucial part of the marketing strategies since villagers have low mobility, less knowledge and familiarity with the urban markets for purchasing negotiations. In the second phase of their marketing strategies the focus should be to,

(vi) enhance their purchasing power by providing micro-credit,

(vii) through micro-credit, businesses also capture some share of market for regular products and services in course of time thus increasing their total market share.

Another peculiarity of the rural market will be the fast changing consumer scenarios due to their exposure to media channels of TV where they are exposed to life styles of various Indian regions and the world around.

Network Effect Business Model. Network effects were used as justification for some of the business models for dot-coms in the late 1990s. These firms operated under the belief that when a new market comes into being which contains strong network effects, companies should care more about growing their market share than about becoming profitable. This was believed because market share will determine which company can set technical and marketing standards and thus determine the basis of future competition.

Network effects become significant after a certain subscription percentage has been achieved, called *critical mass*. At the critical mass point, the value obtained from the goods or services is greater than or equal to the price paid for the goods or services. As the user base determines the value of the goods, this implies that after a certain number of people have subscribed to the service or purchased the goods, additional people will subscribe to the service or purchase the goods due to the positive utility — price ratio. Until this point has been achieved, however, only early adopters will subscribe.

One consequence of a network effect is that the purchase of goods by one individual indirectly benefits others who own the goods — for example by purchasing a telephone a person makes other telephones more useful. This type of side effect in a transaction is known as an externality in economics, and externalities arising from network effects are known as network externalities.

The increasing number of subscribers cannot continue indefinitely. After a certain point, most networks become either congested or saturated, stopping future uptake. Congestion occurs due to overuse. The applicable analogy is that of a telephone network. While the number of users is below the congestion point, each additional user adds additional value to every other customer. However, at some point the addition of an extra user exceeds the capacity of the existing system. After this point, each additional user decreases the value obtained by every other user. In practical terms, each additional user increases the total system load, leading to busy signals, the inability to get a dial tone, and poor customer support. The next critical point is where the value obtained equals the price paid again. *The network will cease to grow at this point, and the system must be enlarged.* The congestion point may be larger than the market size. New Peer-to-Peer technological models may always defy congestion. Peer-to-Peer systems, or "P2P," are networks designed to distribute load among their user pool. This theoretically allows true P2P networks to scale indefinitely. But market saturation will still occur.

Network effects are commonly mistaken for economies of scale, which result from business size rather than interoperability. To help clarify the distinction, people speak of demand side vs. supply side economies of scale. Classical economies of scale are on the production side, while network effects arise on the demand side. Network effects are also mistaken for economies of scope.

Examples, ***Software:*** There are very strong network effects operating in the market for widely-used computer software. Take for example, Microsoft Office, for many people choosing an office suite; prime considerations include, how valuable having learned that office suite will prove to potential employers, and how well the software interoperates with other users, since learning to use an office suite takes many hours, they want to invest that time, learning the office suite, which will make them most attractive to potential employers (or consulting clients, etc), and they also want to be able to share documents with potential co-workers. Similarly, finding already-trained employees is a big concern for employers when deciding which office suite to purchase or standardize on. The lack of cross-platform standards results in a situation in which one company is in control of almost 100% of the market.

However, network effects need not lead to market dominance by one company, when there are standards that allow multiple companies to interoperate, thus allowing the network externalities to benefit the entire market. This is true for the case of x86-based personal computer hardware, in which there are extremely strong market pressures to interoperate with pre-existing standards, but in which no one company dominates in the market. The same holds true for the market for long-distance telephone service within the United States. In fact, the existence of these types of networks discourages dominance of the market by one company, as it creates pressures that work against one company attempting to establish a proprietary protocol or to even distinguish itself by means of product differentiation.

In cases in which the relevant communication protocols are under the control of a single company, however, the network effect can give the company monopoly power. The Microsoft Corporation is widely seen by computer professionals as maintaining its monopoly through these means. One observed method Microsoft uses to put the network effect to its advantage is called embrace and extend (derisively called embrace, extend, and extinguish).

A limited handful of *websites* also feature a network effect. Generally, web marketplaces and exchanges feature a network effect, in that the value of the marketplace to a new user is proportional to the number of other users in the market. For example, eBay would not be a particularly useful site if auctions were not competitive. However, as the numbers of users grew on eBay, auctions grew more competitive, pushing up the prices of bids on items. This made it more worthwhile to sell on eBay and brought more sellers onto eBay, which drove prices down again as this increased supply and also brought more people onto eBay because there were things being sold that people wanted. Essentially, as the number of users of eBay grew, the prices reflected better supply-and-demand and more and more people found the site to be useful.

The collaborative encyclopedia Wikipedia also benefits from a network effect. As the number of editors grows, the quality of information on the website improves, encouraging more users to turn to it as a source of information; many of the new users in turn became editors and continuing the process.

Social networking websites are also good examples. The more people registered onto a social networking website, the more useful the website is to its registrants. By contrast, the value of a news site is primarily proportional to the quality of the articles, not to the number of other people using the site. Similarly, the first generation of search sites experienced little network effect, as the value of the site was based on the value of the search results. This allowed Google to win users away from Yahoo! Without much trouble, once users believed that Google's search results were superior. Some commentators mistook the value of the Yahoo brand (which does increase as more people know of it) for a network effect protecting its advertising business.

Google has also attempted to create a network effect in its advertising business with its Google AdSense service. It places ads along the relevant news or other matter. Google AdSense places ads on many small sites, such as blogs, using Google technology to determine which ads are relevant to which blogs. Thus, the service appears to aim to serve as an exchange (or ad network) for matching many advertisers with many small sites (such as blogs). In general, the more blogs Google AdSense can reach, the more advertisers it will attract, making it the most attractive option for more blogs, and so on, making the network more valuable for all participants.

Network effects and technology lifecycle: If some existing technology or company whose benefits are largely based on network effects starts to lose market share against a challenger such as a disruptive technology or open standards based competition, the benefits of network effects will reduce for the incumbent, and increase for the challenger. In this model, a tipping point is eventually reached at which the network effects of the challenger dominate those of the former incumbent, and the incumbent is forced into an accelerating decline, whilst the challenger takes over the incumbent's former position.

Outsourcing and Offshore Business Models are now open to new combinations of outsourcing, service providers, and off shoring. The outcomes of such business models are: globalization, global delivery models, multi-country supplier and delivery models, hub-and-spoke model in globalization of services, captive centers model, small and medium enterprises using off shoring. There are product development and design facilities offshoring model, the 'Second wave' model for expertise-driven jobs and iGen consumerism model in outsourced countries and the reverse outsourcing model.

There are Intercultural learning and training models including language facility, mannerisms, and ways of handling situations both in business and social set ups, business culture learning and training models of both outsourced and outsourcing companies in different countries. They are offshoots of outsourcing and creating business and business models of different kind.

The developed countries are outsourcing their various business processes to developing countries because of cheaper costs and thus more profitability. The capabilities, which are outsourced offshore, have moved from IT-centric functions into business processes. The complexity of these capabilities continues to climb with functions such as patent research, drug research and development, legal services and equity research beginning to emerge as the high-end of offshore outsourcing. There are services such as data entry, technical support and financial analytics, which require vastly different skill sets, end up being lumped together and evaluated as "offshore business process services."

Educated English speaking younger age manpower, IT centric trained personnel, low labor costs, growing infrastructure, suitability of time zones and willingness of business and the government to regulate and facilitate outsourcing to developing countries. Broad categories like people skills and availability; business environment, and financial structure facilitate it further. Apart from cyber security, other issues that are critical to growth of IT are infrastructure and human resources. For example, India has depth and breadth of technologically skilled labor available at a low cost; English language skills that facilitate communications with the developed English-speaking countries; an improving telecommunications infrastructure and extensive IT experience.

Different developing countries have different outsourcing strengths such as India has more IT centric, software development strengths. China has manufacturing strength both garments and hardware mechanical devices. Stiff competition is growing up among countries with high or low strengths as outsourcing product and services scope is widening.

However, while complexity is increasing, respective cost expectations are not shifting accordingly. But selling BPO services is becoming tougher and tougher as clients get more knowledgeable about outsourcing and competition increases with an ever-growing number of players.

Increasing acceptance for off-shoring is a foregone conclusion for multinational corporations that must keep pace with global competition, global supply and global delivery models. The role of offshore outsourcing will continue to grow in importance as off-shoring moves to a corporate "must have" and as companies develop more sophisticated global delivery models across IT and multiple business processes, e.g. General Electric's recent spin-off of its India BPO unit. We also predict the emergence of multi-country supplier and delivery models that span the globe from India to China to central Europe. In the client market, US companies will no longer be the dominant buyers as western European firms create strong demand for offshore services. A longer list of contenders will only reflect the rapidly spreading interest around the world in getting a piece of the BPO action. Off shoring will grow in size and complexity as clients leverage on early lessons.

While the amount of back-office work that is currently sent outside their national borders by Western, European and Japanese companies is still a tiny fraction of the total amount of such work that these companies outsource. Still it constitutes a substantial source of revenue and employment for recipient countries, as India has demonstrated.

Despite GE's spin-off, the increasing complexity of processes being off-shored will lead to more wholly owned offshore subsidiaries for BPO, often referred to as captive centers. Existing captive shared services centers will become targets for further efficiency and expansion. It predicts that over 40% of offshore initiatives will not yield anticipated savings, scale or risk diversification. The key reason for these disappointments will not be due to supplier capability but buyer preparation and management.

In 2006 the expectation is that small and medium enterprises will finally be clients for off shoring as they weigh the benefits of off-shoring due to budget pressures and a more accepting political environment for off shoring.

The next big emerging phenomenon is a hub-and-spoke model in globalization of services. Singapore already has become a BPO off-shoring hub whose spokes extend to India, China and the Philippines, and some day could reach out to Sri Lanka and Vietnam. Dubai has the potential to be a Singapore-like hub in the Middle East. It is stable, forward looking and technological advanced. While the role of BPO hub by definition will be reserved to a chosen few locations, the spokes are likely to proliferate. It is as much about labor availability as it is about cost.

A 'second wave' seems to be coming in off shoring of business processes in which English language fluency will not be a decisive factor. These will be expertise-driven jobs, requiring mainly the ability to analyze and solve complex problems.

For example, these workers may be involved in bioinformatics, or risk analytics for insurance, or scenario management in sell-side equity research, and then, someone in the US can wrap the English language around their work.

Some businesses are off shoring product development and design facilities. The problem with it is that technology will leak out to local competitors. For companies that rely on cutting-edge innovation, protecting intellectual property is critical especially as local competitors are also going up the technology ladder.

There is outgrowing trend of reverse outsourcing also. Bharti telecommunication, India's premier telecom has outsourced its maintenance of its telecom infrastructure to IBM and Siemens who have set up business facilities in India (Gurgaon) to service it (2004-05). This trend is likely to grow worldwide.

China comes second owing to its cheap and plentiful labor supply and fast-improving infrastructure, but lags behind India because of its relative lack of English skills, cultural barriers and a weak legal system. Overall, Asian companies dominate the rankings, occupying six of the top ten locations.

Remote infrastructural management (RIM) is the new wave in India. It is done through an offshore operations center that monitors and manages the infrastructure, ensuring guaranteed uptimes, availability and enhanced performance. Currently, RIM business out of India is nearly $200 to $300 and by the end of 2006 may surpass $1 billion. However, the global market for such outsourcing job is between $86 billion and $150 billion. As RIM catches up in India, thousands jobs get created. Companies are opting for RIM as international connectivity and bandwidth into India is relatively easy now. Therefore managing servers and providing production support can be delivered effectively over a global network.

The Economist Intelligence Unit's ranking model measures the attractiveness of 60 countries as destinations for off shoring, scoring each country on nine criteria commonly used by companies when deciding where to offshore. Countries were scored on labor costs, labor skills, labor regulation, proximity to major sources of investment, political and security risk, macroeconomic stability, regulatory environment, tax regime and infrastructure. "With outsourcing and off-shoring becoming critical forces for business, it is important that businesses look internally both at their motivation for off shoring and their ability to manage such a function,' said Andrew Briggs, Dimension Data's head of contact centers business. "Off-shoring cannot fix broken processes but in fact may only serve to exacerbate the problems, irrespective of the location chosen," he added.

Outsourcing Model for high end: To be precise, global consumer electronic majors are now launching many of their latest innovations in India, much ahead of even the US, Europe and Japan. For example, Hitachi recently launched a range of 32 to 42-inch plasma TV models in India, the second country in Asia after Singapore. Samsung introduced their 'Pleomax' range of IT products here just after their South Korea launch. Electrolux global launch of 'talking' washing machine included India. The trend is now really picking-up. A few like LG, Philips and Electrolux are even significantly investing on developing features and technologies largely suited for India. They have realized that the domestic consumer is no more price-conscious and is ready to pay for superior technology. Quite naturally, there is a mad rush by the companies to enjoy the first-mover advantage.

"The market is showing a swift shift from low-end and mid-end segments to high-end, and the first one to invest will ultimately drive the volumes," Electrolux India's vice-president (sales and marketing), told *Economic Times*. Currently, about 60% of product innovations at Electrolux are targeted at the Indian markets. "There is a growing demand for premium audio and visual products in the Indian market. Hitachi wants to carve a distinct niche for itself and has, as a policy, identified India as a priority market," said Tadashi Nishiuchi, managing director, Hitachi Home Electronics Asia.

Interestingly, the companies are also relying on premium products to drive their brand values. "With extremely high pressure on bottom line, every company is now striving to derive higher brand values with latest technologies. It ultimately boosts the sales of low and medium product segments as well". Efforts are on to develop the market for premium products

Some of the challenges of outsourcing: Companies make the decision to outsource after careful strategic planning and review of the pros and cons of each scenario. They chose either a third party outsource company or set up their own facility in host country — say India. Companies invest time, resources (including people) and have a few key executives to manage the operation, on the ground. These people are now responsible for managing the operational challenges in India in context of its business cultures and social cultures; and creating challenges of culture learning.

There are political and economic ramifications from outsourcing/offshoring countries, for example in US when people are losing jobs to other countries. But there were 100 sectors where there were no job losses associated with service outsourcing. This, according to them, implies that a worker could lose his/her job due to outsourcing, but may later find a job in another firm within the broader industry classification.

Hence, they conclude that there are no net job losses when there is sufficient job creation in another sector, which indeed seems to be the case. They contend that even if outsourcing leads to some shedding of labor, increased efficiency could lead to higher production and an expansion of employment in other lines of work. Share of imports of "private services" — educational, financial, insurance, telecommunications, business, professional, technical and others — from developing countries to the US, though increasing, is still quite low at 32%. The remaining 68% originates in other industrial countries.

The other social challenges for outsourced countries are to handle the consumerism among younger generations who are able to earn more at a fairly young age. Though such consumerism is creating markets and boosting economy of the host countries.

INFORMATION ECONOMY MANAGEMENT

New business models both in domestic markets and in global contexts do facilitate economic growth through increasing economic concerns, focuses and choices. The information society progresses to the advance stage through development of information technology culture and its diffusion. This has impact on economy at national and international levels and facilitates gaining power. Managing of information is of increasing concerns to the organizations: how to make a whole of the scattered information, how to screen out relevant information and how to extract from the information environment those messages which are likely to have significance for the organizations.

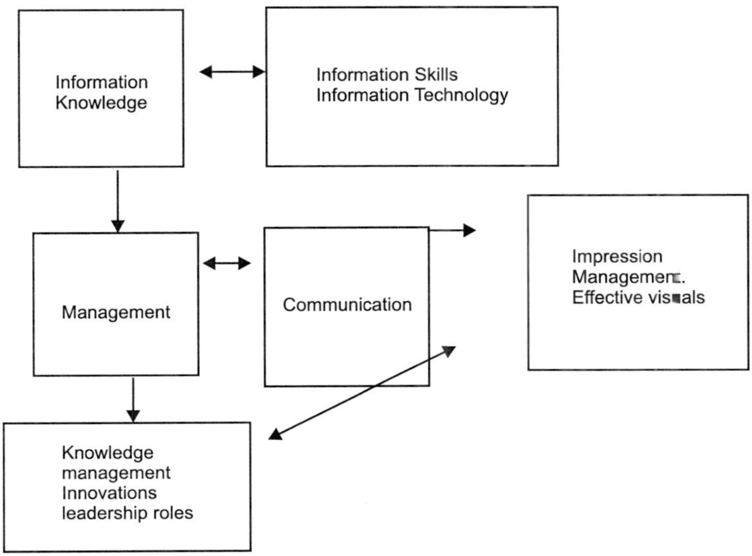

Fig. 5.10. Global Information Economy Management

It is important to manage the three business components i.e. business dimensions, business intelligence and social components, and applications of ICTs efficiently. Business intelligence and its social components, changing dimensions and areas of businesses, and the new and wider applications of ICTs create a specific business culture for a particular business. Communications through conventional and new media technologies, and interpersonal channels play significant role in managing these three business communication components. Internet and various modes of mobile communications have facilitated global business and globalization in business.

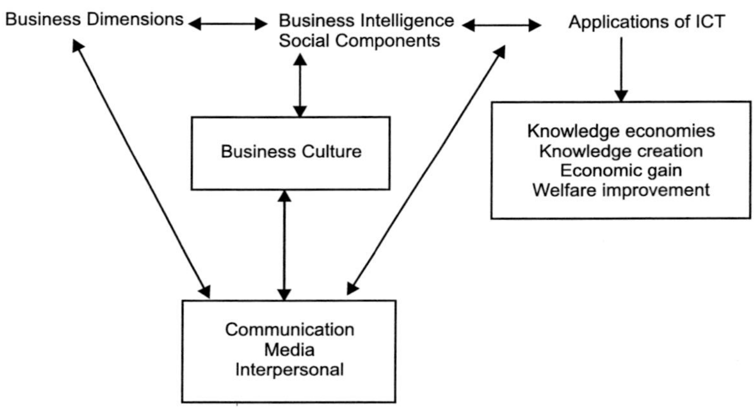

Fig. 5.11. Business Communication Management

Knowledge as an important component of communications needs management for its effective use in any sector of activity. This model addresses the issues of knowledge management competencies and dynamics, various components, applications, techniques, and its impact on number of variables. Managing knowledge economies is efficient use of knowledge for economic gains and improving the wellbeing of people both socially and materially. Efficient use of knowledge through dynamic information infrastructure and assimilation of global knowledge create educated and skilled work force. Assimilation of global knowledge stimulates e-readiness, k-readiness and innovations. Knowledge growth linkages and policies of particular countries further enhance the economic growth and well being of its people.

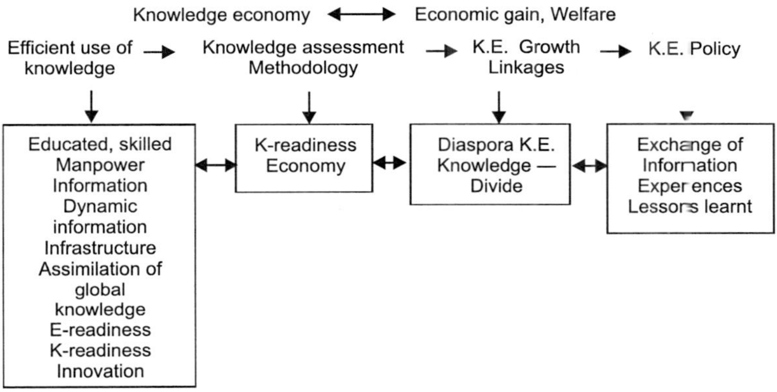

Fig. 5.12. Managing Knowledge Economies

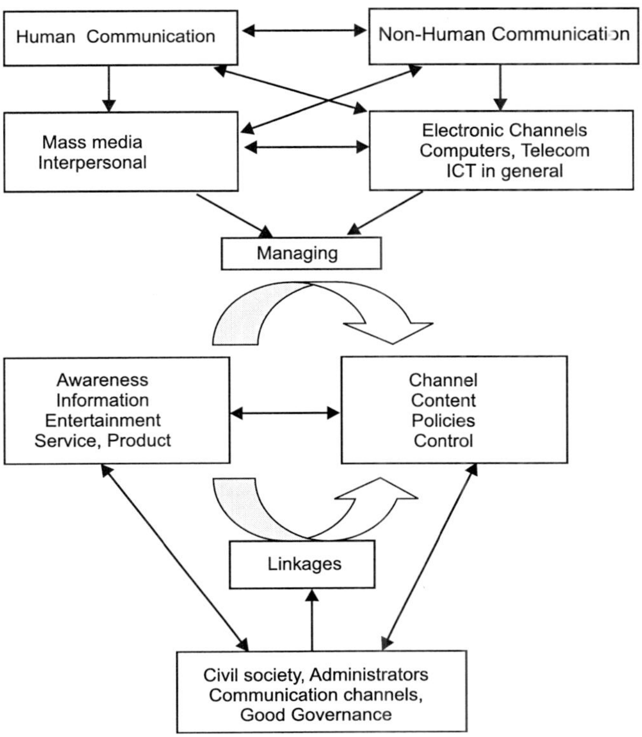

Fig. 5.13. Communication Management Competence

BUSINESS COMMUNICATION PRACTICES

Business enterprise has three basic functions — Innovations, Marketing and Communications. The various business practices relate to these three functions.

These produce results. Thus in any business enterprise marketing and communications are the two major tools for innovations of products and services.

There is a paradigm shift from the past in the business practices of today, and the same can be expected for the future. It is equally true of emerging economies of India and China or the developed world. The trends in how people do business around the world are changing; there is globalization of business practices as the businesses themselves are getting globalized. Developed countries are outsourcing manufacturing; IT & IT enabled services from companies in developing countries like China and India. However, business practices are still unique to a particular country within the globalization framework, because of its cultural ways and values.

We define business practice as not just producing, marketing and delivering products and services for economic gains (capital development) but they also include the practices of human development, social responsibility (in business contexts), and business etiquettes. Therefore, leaders planning to do business in alien country must understand and relate well to the business practices, business cultures of the particular business in general, and to the bureaucratic and government practices of dealing with businesses.

Historically, robust communication channels and timely flow of critical content have been the key enablers for successful business enterprises. Globalization, technology and economic liberalization are changing the business practices and how they are communicated. There is a paradigm shift both in business contexts, models, practices and business communication models and practices. We cannot deny the importance and significance of how MICE (media, information, communication and entertainment) technologies are contributing as well changing the business practices. Many of the business models today and in the future are possible because of the new channels and modes of communication.

Business practices and communications both human and non-human (technological) are intertwined. Business transactions occur in every human activity — be it be big or small. There is little difficulty in identifying a particular instance of social action as *Communication.* The problem arises in specifying what human actions are *not communications.* From these perspectives, many social actions that otherwise would not be defined as instances of communication, are shown to be powerful means of creating and managing business reality. The complexity in interaction results from human and non-human communications.

Business relates to markets for any product and services. Products essentially relate to tangible goods, and the services are either the by-product of these tangible goods and allied to them, and are essential for delivery of products. It is a wide term being used for all categories of businesses such as consumer goods and services of durable and non-durables, banking, insurances, hospitals, schools, real estate, travel, stock markets etc. Further, these are classified into segmented markets for different classes of people who do consume but differently, and have the capacity to pay differently such as — poor, middle class, elite class etc. There are different geographic areas such as urban and rural that determines the patterns of consumptions and the market demands. There are different cultural groups globally who also determine the market segments. These differentiations create different business dealings.

There are business theories and concepts, paradigms and guidelines that give a general framework for businesses to operate in any market. We do need specific approaches, models and guidelines to deal with differentiated markets. These specifics change with the times, business and technology moves, as well with the changing characteristics of the customers and consumers.

Businesses communication deal with the core competencies of people, processes and technology. Interpersonal communication is essential and is used significantly in business. Technologies of computer, telecommunication, satellites, and other information communication technologies and other auto-ID business technologies such as evolutionary technologies of Bar Code and RFID are predominant on the communication scenario. These provide technological solutions for business processes.

Globalizations, technology and economic liberalization have tremendously changed the business practices worldwide. Business practices have to keep pace with the rapid technological change to be successful. Best practices of yesterday may not serve the consumers of today; therefore the practices are on a continuum of change. Three models of Globalism, Glocalization and Outsourcing in the context of Globalization may profile business practices differently. Globalism is the awareness that local events have global consequences and understanding of global impact. Glocalization is merging local and global trends. This model operates in two ways: one is adapting and fitting global trends to local ways such as fitting global business practices to local business cultures. Second, local trends are changed into global trends. Such as business practices are changed to global practices of doing business.

The emerging economies are booming because of these three factors — globalization, technology and economic liberalization. Further models of *Globalism* and *Glocalization* shape the focus of their business, products and services. In addition, they are competitive and achieve more when they follow a *Collaborative model* of Business Communication practices. Catering to *Low-end Mass Market* is new upcoming business practice in the emerging markets.

It is an observation that different emerging markets have their business strengths and weaknesses according to their specific models of business communication practices. Some of these are emerging as booming markets as interplay of abovementioned three factors and other additional models but their markets develop according to models of their predominant business strengths. As such emerging markets of China and India are taking different paths to economic prosperity as per their business strengths.

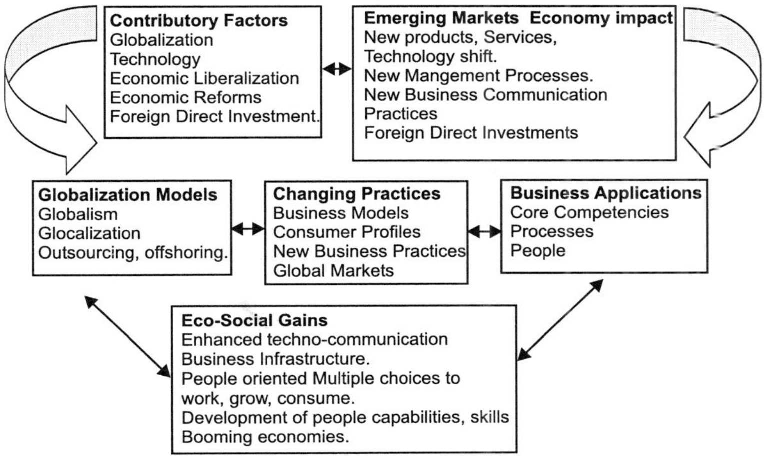

Fig. 5.14. Impact of Changing Business Practices

6

Governance and People

PARTICIPATORY DEVELOPMENT AND GOOD GOVERNANCE MODEL

A productive, just and humane, participatory society is aimed at through democratic way of discourses and dialogues. Community voices are heard, their concerns are addressed, and solutions are found and implemented through discourses and dialogues. Participation of all is the essential and important key.

The focus is on strengthening the partnership approach to participatory development and good governance. This has radical implication for world economy. The emphasis is on micro level action contexts, local resistance to change, community participation, and empowerment of people through participation.

Economic and political liberalism is necessary for PDGG model. It is necessary that there should be vital connection between open, democratic, and accountable political systems, individual rights, and effective and equitable operations of economic systems with substantial reduction of poverty.

The Participatory Development and Good Governance (PDGG) model addresses the role of multinationals in developing socio-economic development; growing global disparities; and the importance of dialogue between government and civil society actors. In globalization of the world, there is no symmetry and congruency between political and economic decision-makers and political and economic decision receivers. Thus there is widening of marginalization and deepening of polarization of world economy culminating in growing global disparities.

Political liberalism aims at establishing accountable system of government through widespread participation of people and respect for human rights. The government is accountable to parliament and there is political decentralization.

We should have good governance participation through honest, intelligent, effective people with involvement. The important dimensions of good governance are rule of the law in the country, public sector is managed effectively and efficiently, controlling corruption, and reducing excessive military expenditure. Worldwide empirical evidence shows that corruption lowers economic growth. The explicit reasons for participation development are:

(a) empowerment of non-government actors on government and their influencing the public policy,

(b) enhancement of efficiency, effectiveness, sustainability of concrete development programs. The misuse of government power creates serious credibility problems whose effects can be encountered long after the event.

We should have good governance through good people. The core issues are: right to elect must be accompanied by right to reject; improve law and order so that families are safe and secure. People want justice and not charity. Address causes of corruption. Corruption is either need based or greed based. What starts as need based becomes greed based.

If we are not part of the solution then we are the problem. A country is wrecked not by the activities of the dishonest people but by the inaction and lethargy of the good and honest people. India is not the first country where there are problematic issues but certainly it is the first one which does not seek to redress them. Even after independence we are still suffering because we vote and choose our political representatives by casting votes in the name of caste and religion rather than on principles.

Our problems of today are the result of our past shortsighted solutions. If you vote for third rate political leaders then not only you do not trust them; but you are bargaining with them the future of the country. Bad leaders take money from the rich and vote from the poor on the promise that they will protect both. A society is in danger when those who have never learned to obey are given the right to command. Good political leaders serve the country but third rate leaders get personal benefits from the country. Political coalitions not based on principles only circulate the inefficient and does not let the qualified and efficient leaders come up.

Public opinion is valuable but a country is bound to go down and suffer where rash public opinion has more value than justice and principles. Injustice and unjust administration is organized exploitation. A citizen who values more on his privileges than on principles loses both. A society depends more on the character of its citizens rather than on their intelligence alone. A citizen can never die or live with dignity in a corrupt country. A dishonest person always thinks twisted ways are the right ways. Good people live for others but bad people live on others. Future paves the way for those with strong determination but drags those who have wrong determinations.

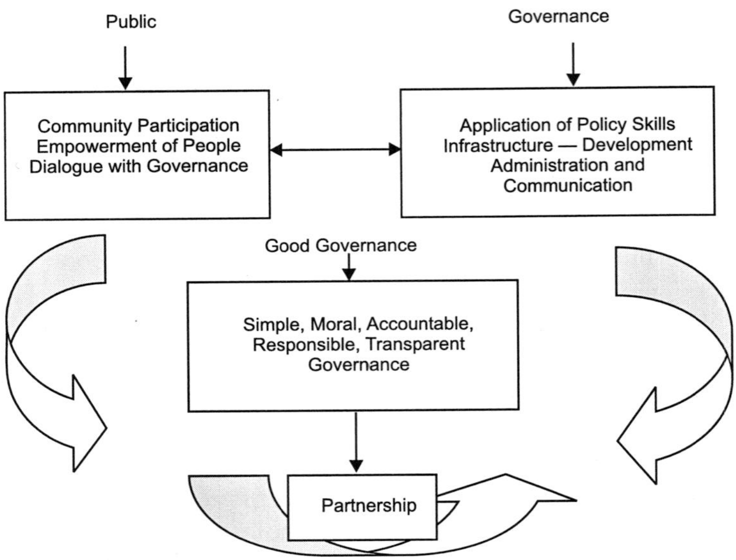

Fig. 6.1. Participatory Development and Good Governance Model

Narula (2006c) points that Development Economists concentrate on the quality of the development process. More important is how economic growth is used to improve human capabilities and their utilization. Politics and economics are intertwined. From this perspective, a planned change of values, attitudes, and behaviors of individuals in developing countries becomes necessary. The emphasis is on the development of human manpower to fit modernity roles. Further, the local social structure is not just an obstacle to overcome for modernization but a context from which development activities derive their meaning and significance. The communication practices for human development is through participatory communication.

The communication practices are changing for Participatory Development and Good Governance (PDGG) model. The focus is discourses, dialogues with communities in multiple contexts. A productive, just and humane, participatory society is aimed at through democratic way of discourses and dialogues. Community voices are heard, their concerns are addressed, and solutions are found and implemented through discourses and dialogues. The chosen options and its consequences are addressed through discourses and negotiated through dialogues and multilogues of various actors involved.

DISCOURSES AND DIALOGUE STRATEGIES

Dialogue strategies for development are necessary for PDGG model. The emphasis is on micro level action contexts, local resistance to change, community participation, and empowerment of people through participation. SMART (simple, moral, accountable and transparent) government is advocated for development. Discourses and Dialogue strategies for development can be built around a development issue through the two components of participation and good governance. Discourses on public issues must set the agenda for dialogue strategies between the public and the governance. Through the process of discourses and dialogue strategies; the government knows the needs of people and the people know the limitations of government; and they agree to do development within the framework of partnership.

There is bound to be gap between pledges and programs, goals and accomplishments by the governance. There is bound to be gap between the efforts of governance in planning and implementation of economic policies due to constrains of resources as well as willingness of the Political will. This could be challenging. But people's participation is imperative in demanding that pledges and goals be accomplished; and that right kind of economic policies are planned for economic prosperity of people. But demanding itself is not sufficient. What are necessary are people's efforts, motivation and participation in implementing and achieving those goals in collaboration with governance. It is the combined efforts of the people and governance that will transform Visions — of both people and governance in Reality. That is the challenge that both people and governance must face. Thus people cannot be totally dependent on governance if they want economic prosperity; and governance cannot ignore the Visions of its people. Good governance is partnership between government and people.

7

Epilogue

INDIA EMERGING AND SURGING

Our discussions in the foregone chapters have highlighted the Indian economic scenario vis-à-vis economic visions, technology visions and the business visions of its people, its governance and commitment of both to make it reality by facing the ensuing challenges in national as well as globalization contexts. The people and government face these challenges in order to enjoy better quality of life both in national and globalization contexts as they have envisioned. It is not always the bigger issues of globalization or expanding businesses worldwide that will impact our economic growth and prosperity but also to what extent the population is provided minimum needs of life in reality; and the attitude of people and government to procure it efficiently. This is more challenging for Indian economy.

Our visions start with ideology always; therefore our economic visions are also ideal and real as well. We have to start with ideal and fit that with reality by planning and policy. Ideology focuses on objectives — both short and long terms goals of overall development. Planning should focus on resources and policies to achieve these goals. Reality is achievement through implementation.

Our economic visions should be functional and they could be made successful. The ultimate success of the visions lies in improving quality of human life. Our visions can be made successful by efforts of governance and people, economists and businesses.

Achievement can occur if there is efficiency in economic management. This requires involved efforts of the governance and people. ***It is important how people and governance communicate their visions to each other.***

People have certain ideology of development based on their own values, aspirations, and expectations from planners and development functionaries for economic growth. Governance and people both must meet challenges of economic reforms in India to fulfill the visions of economic prosperity of country and its people.

Configurations of change are created overtime according to the inputs of the economists, businesses, governance and people and also interaction of these variables in varied permutations. Communication plays significant role in how these inputs and interactions are created. Communication messages, channels handle these concerns to create an equitable society.

The common heuristics are important in understanding the limitations of human economic choices which itself is a social process; such as the Anchor Points from which people start out when making a judgment. Reference to Anchor points is important to understand assumptions that individuals have about their entitlements, obligations, and opportunities in a society.

The ideological commitment at the political level is important for shaping the economic policies and choices. The political leaders set salient economic priorities for its people. Narula (1994 — 1999) points that public opinion and the political system in India symbolize the complex strands of idealism and selfishness, commitment and dismay, planning and bureaucracy, blame and self-justification, and overwhelming discontent that comprise current Indian economic development.

The main challenge is to provide economic and social opportunities to people by streamlining economic policies. How they are planned, implemented and delivered through the combined efforts of people, governance and international agencies and institutions is imperative for fulfillment of its economic visions and its economic growth.

India needs to find ways to harness the full creative capability of its inhabitants across all industries, occupations, classes and geo regions. This would give India an advantage in the global creative economy and provide the world with a large-scale model for how development of human capabilities is the most effective route to true economic development.

Managing knowledge economies is efficient use of knowledge for economic gains and improving the wellbeing of people both socially and materially. Knowledge growth linkages and policies of particular countries further enhance the economic growth and well being of its people. New business models both in domestic markets and in global contexts does facilitate economic growth through increasing economic concerns, focuses and choices. The information society progresses to the advance stage through development of information technology culture and its diffusion. This has impact on economy at national and international levels and facilitates gaining power.

Market forces alone cannot determine economic future. Each country determines and draws a road map for economic reforms that would be based on its own skills, resources, strengths and vulnerabilities. To expect developing countries to continually liberalize, at an extreme pace, even within a rule based regime, may result in opposite of what is desirable.

Different emerging markets including India have their business strengths and weaknesses according to their specific models of business communication practices. Their markets develop according to models of their predominant business strengths. The competencies of Indian people at all levels, has made India a global player in many businesses and has boosted the business image as well economy of India.

India is doing efficiently and cautiously both — *opening up businesses* for outsourcing, economic liberalization and FDI; *and opening the society.* These two can develop in parallel. *That is how India envisions its problem and development — Emerging and Surging.*

GLOBALIZATION TRENDS: CHANGING BUSINESS PRACTICES

We present our concluding observations about the changing business practices that impact the growth of economy in different countries. Globalizations, technology and economic liberalization have tremendously changed the business practices worldwide. These three factors have tremendously changed the consumer profile — consumer behavior, preferences, demands and expectations for products and services from housing to consumer durables and non-durables and as diverse fields as insurance, sanitation and legal systems. Thus consumer is the focus from manufacturing to medical services to education services. There is a Paradigm shift to new business practices in these and many new areas. New business practices can be observed in earlier conventional areas and practices and in the upcoming new segments.

There are upcoming New Practices. Change is a process and there is continuity of the earlier. Earlier change becomes history. What was earlier best practice is no longer so. It is outdated. Nonetheless, we do learn our lessons from the history of change and best practices and move on to bring more change for the better and new. Those who keep pace with the changing do progress, but who do not stagnate. Same way, businesses need to change the business practices to match the changing consumer profiles. Globalization and technology make the consumer profiles change rapidly as they are exposed to newer trends. Technology innovates as well re-innovates to set these new trends. Business practices have to keep pace with the rapid technological change to be successful. Best practices of yesterday may not serve the consumers of today; the practices are on a continuum of change — sometimes positive and sometimes negative. Therefore, even the businesses have to be selective and competitive about which practices will give them edge.

Business practices, business models and consumer profiles have changed. There are more *collaborative efforts* in doing businesses. In fact, there is global supply chain whether in setting the fashion design such as supplying clothes, clothes designing, buttons and other accessories, stitching, clothing models and consumers apart from the marketing processes; or for manufacturing the cars or even setting up medical or educational services. Collaborative efforts call for communication, co-ordination, (through one-on-one, group meeting, business presentations, conferences and regional or world focused summits), problem-solving, decision-making and applied creativity to find creative solutions. *These days beside the capital development, human capital development both at local and global level is also of utmost importance from the point of globalization of business practices.*

The business technology and personal technology is going to change the communication between the customers, consumers and different layers of management. Since the customers/consumers are getting more and more informed about the business channels, products and services and they would be making informed demands, and critic and reject any products and services not up-to-mark. Their preferences and expectations will change fast because of fast exposure to information and that also at global level. The communication styles and message focus among employees at different layers of management and top leaders will go tremendous change due to being well-informed about the changing ways of doing things at business, expected to have different relationship with the customers and services because of changing products and services. The changes will be further supported and upgraded by the business technology both in dealing with the products and services and information for the employees, management layers and top-leaders; and the supply chain customers and consumers.

What is update today in business communication may be redundant and outdated and the search for the new will be ongoing.

Globalization gives ambitious companies access to the best capital, talent, markets, and resources that the world has to offer. But then companies are essentially competing against the best in the world. The changing landscape will force many companies to reevaluate their strengths and weaknesses. As the pace of globalization accelerates, companies will no longer be able to take advantages or protectionist regulation. Competitors will need to restructure their organizations to match the skills of the world's best players.

As capital markets and markets in goods and services become more international, economies must respond to pressures that are not under the control of nation state. New technologies assist this process, allowing for the integration of production processes and swifter exchange of information. International capital shifts must be seen as of fundamental importance.

In reality, *the process of global economic integration* — of which offshore outsourcing is a highly visible component — *diffuses the best business ideas and management tools, intensifies competition, and sparks innovation.* It thereby leads to lower prices and higher wages as well as bigger profits that companies can reinvest in new business opportunities. The fact that economic integration benefits the global economy as a whole doesn't mean that it benefits all workers and companies.

Models of Globalism, Glocalization and Outsourcing in the context of Globalization may profile business practices differently. Globalism discourse is based on three levels: values, knowledge and interests. The focus is on global understanding and global consciousness. *It is the awareness that local events have global consequences and understanding of global impact.* Globalism suggests a global culture of standardization of food, clothes, music, TV programs, films, business practices etc. Global has two meanings: One, is the traditional definition of international, which has messages, data, or people going across or through some kind of barriers, boundaries or constraints, whether it be the encoding or decoding process from one human being to other, or the artificial borders between nation-states. *The other definition concerns issues that are common enough to group of people to transcend traditional boundaries.*

Glocalization is merging local and global trends. This model operates in two ways: One, adapting and fitting global trends to local ways such as fitting global business practices to local business cultures. There is more localization and picking only the relevant. Second, local trends are changed into global trends. Such as, business practices are changed to global practices of doing business.

Outsourcing of manufacturing of products and services and knowledge based industries moved initially from western countries to countries where cost of production is low and professional competency is available as in knowledge-based industries. Profit making is the main driving force for outsourcing. As we observe, the outsourcing model has changed overtime in the context of demands, opportunities, technology innovations and interdependency of countries and impact of globalism and glocalization models.

INDIAN ECONOMIC SCENARIO: VISIONS AND REALITY

Globalizations, technology and economic liberalization and economic reforms, economic policies allowing foreign direct investment (FDI) in Indian enterprises have tremendously changed both business, and business communication practices in India. India is exposed to global business practices through technology and other channels facilitating globalization.

The Models of Globalism and Glocalization are operative in this context. In 90s India was getting conscious of the fact that local events such as outsourcing and IT hubs will have global consequences and impact. It did value those business propositions, it did create interest among the business community for its economic potential and developed knowledge-based capabilities in the IT areas. Thus Globalism has helped India's exposure to global business practices in the context of global offshore outsourcing and accepting them in their business models and in consequences getting global business partners. It modeled these outsourcing business services on Glocalization model by employing the local capabilities and human talents. It further enhanced the capability and appropriate communication skills of the personnel by utilizing local training professional services.

To set up the infrastructure for these services; they did utilize the foreign funding but it was developed and built by Indian professionals. Thus Glocalization gives Indian businesses chance to cash on their strengths and business cultures. They had strength in IT software applications and development, so they are encashing on that strength and have not so far got into hardware manufacturing of IT that is not its strength as yet. They further strengthen their weakness; such as they needed the foreign funding to set up update infrastructure for outsourcing business.

India's outsourcing model focused on three areas: Customer care through call centers, BPOs for back office professional services and applications, KPOs for knowledge services and products and development of Information Technology services. India has the advantage of graduate, English speaking huge manpower of youngsters who are ready to join call centers after being trained by the local professional trainers. There is huge pool of appropriate professionals such as chartered accountants, medical technicians, radiographers etc. for BPO services. India has well trained IT professionals for outsourcing services in IT areas. The good point is that India is delivering efficient services in these areas to the global partners and creating potential for getting more outsourcing.

Such business practices have created higher employment, higher wages, core competencies and business processes. People have been the main focus and through this process they have gained economically, in competencies, and better life styles promoted through more purchasing power and consumerism with high spend. Interestingly, these growing businesses practices are communicating different lifestyles, economic and social values to young growing generation — the iGen.

The wealth generated by India's fast-growing information technology and business-process-outsourcing industries shows that the country has started living up to its economic potential. By contrast, most sectors of India's economy earlier remained shielded from global competition by high tariffs and restrictions on foreign direct investment and were thus woefully uncompetitive. Although some might argue that removing these barriers would threaten social objectives such as the protection of jobs and incomes, a robust economy would be more likely to realize them. If India is to replicate the success of its IT and outsourcing industries elsewhere in its economy, its leaders must lower barriers to trade and encourage foreign investment in many other sectors.

India's $1.5 billion outsourcing business in 2004/05 illustrates how foreign investment and trade have benefited the country. Along with IT and software, business-process outsourcing is perhaps the most open sector. In 2006 more and more focus is on developing KPO (knowledge process outsourcing) and RIM (Remote infrastructure management).

Without early investments by Multinational companies, the outsourcing industry probably would never have emerged. The success of these companies demonstrated to the world that the country was a credible offshoring destination. Thousands of local workers were trained by Multinationals and expats also to meet the initial requirements; many of whom transferred their skills to Indian companies that sprang up in response. Although Indian outsourcing firms now control over half of the intensely competitive global IT and back-office outsourcing market, all of the leading ones started as joint ventures or subsidiaries of Multinational companies or were founded by managers who had worked for them.

For many companies, offshore outsourcing is about little more than saving costs on low-skill, labor-intensive activities. Yet the leading offshore outsourcing companies offer their Western clients superior performance in high-skill business operations as well. Computer industry players such as Dell, HP, and Gateway demonstrate that offshore outsourcers can even be used to launch attacks on adjacent product markets. Offshoring is no longer just about call centers and assembling products; it is about Western companies using the sophisticated design and management capabilities of their partners in the developing world to go where they can't go alone.

Economic reforms since 90s in India have changed business practices as well how they are communicated to the Indian people and society. There is greater focus on promoting healthy consumerism. There are more protection and safety clauses built in for the low-end consumers. For instance, through economic reforms, the bank loan and mortgage system, and hire-purchase system is worked out. Many middle class people including the younger generation could now buy cars and houses on easy loans and installments for which earlier they have to wait for years to save, and could have enjoyed those facilities only at the fag end of their lives. Such a changed business practice has communicated to the people — zest for life and higher standard for living. This practice has boosted the automotives businesses and Real Estate businesses. Economic reforms in Stock Market controlled the scams which earlier had ruined the investors. Steps were also taken to protect the low-end investors.

Economic liberalization focused on the relaxing restrictions on import and export of products and services, technologies, and experts and expertise. For example, manufacturing facilities were upgraded in many sectors through such imports and through foreign collaborators. This created better consumer products and services for the domestic consumers at competitive prices and promoting domestic markets. At the same time the manufactured goods were allowed to be exported. This helped in balancing the manufacturing capacity and prices.

It is evident in the sector of cars, now we have variety of cars in the market from utility to luxury cars. Other sectors such as cement, steel, oil and gas exploration, telecommunication equipment and services also benefited from opening of markets. Many Indian food products like meat products and vegetables, canned pickles etc. are being exported to neighboring countries and same way the other food products be it chocolates or special cheese or Pepperoni required for Pizza for the Pizza hut are allowed to be imported. Higher level of global expertise is sought in setting up in new hospital services such as Max, Wockhardt have been set up through collaboration with Harvard medical group Boston.

Following the glocal model, the Indian partners in joint ventures have created local employment, upgraded the business expertise and learnt and applied some of the best business practices. By exporting goods and services to outside markets not only they are utilizing their market capacity, creating economic gains but also created global visibility and competition for their products and services. Joint ventures also created global visibility and scope for further businesses.

In India, over the decade the economic liberalization is done cautiously and gradually to safeguard domestic industries and consumers, and economy of the country. The political factor and business groups lobbying have also influenced it time and again.

Opening of markets through economic liberalization has allowed Indian businesses to have joint ventures with foreign companies. Allowing foreign direct investment (FDI) has been another factor that boosted joint ventures.

New research by the McKinsey Global Institute (2004) indicates that the foreign direct investment that did find its way to India has had an overwhelmingly positive impact. The introduction of foreign competition in IT, business-process outsourcing, and the automotive industry has prompted Indian companies to revamp their operations and boost productivity, and some have become formidable global competitors. Thousands of new jobs have been created in these industries. Consumers benefit from lower prices, better quality, and a wider selection of products and services, while domestic demand has soared in response to lower prices. MGI's latest research shows that the country must go further in lowering trade and foreign-investment barriers if it is to continue integrating itself into the global economy.

The dynamic growth and competitiveness of India's outsourcing and automotive industries stand in contrast to most of its economy, where continuing restrictions on foreign investment and trade dampen competition and help inefficient companies survive. India has clearly benefited from closer integration into the global economy. To build on that success, the government must now lower trade and foreign-investment barriers still further.

Getting the full benefit of foreign investment calls for competition within industries, since it forces companies to improve their operations and innovate. Many forms of protection and regulation can stifle competition and thus limit the impact of foreign investment. The consumer electronics industry is a prime example. Still, the entry of multinational players has boosted the local industry's productivity and given Indian consumers more choices and lower prices.

Despite these gains, consumer electronics goods made in India still can't compete internationally, and the country's consumers pay unduly high prices for them. These same problems limit foreign investment and prevent many industries — including banking, heavy industry, and textiles — from reaching their full potential. Ultimately, consumers and workers pay through higher prices and the lower pace of job creation.

India estimates that it needs hundreds of billions of dollars in investment in infrastructure, power, transportation, and telecommunication over the next decade to ensure rapid economic growth to reduce poverty. In India, FDI flows are vital for industrial growth as technology and foreign exchange can be accessed through such investments. FDI also helps in raising productivity through better management methods and in creating employment opportunities. It promotes growth by facilitating transfer of technology and help in upgrading skills of the workforce.

In general in India, liberalization of rules governing FDI has contributed to FDI flows. But strong economic policies, strengthening of contract enforcement and implementation of contracts, and reduced risk of nationalization will all have positive effects on FDI flows. A better medium term growth prospectus, greater political stability combined with sound economic policies and continued economic reform process and a heightened tempo of restructuring activities will help India become a desired destination for FDI.

Indian government has cautious policy for FDI also. It has been allowing it in sectors for national priority such as in improving Infrastructure — building of roads, bridges, highways and underground train transportation, and for oil gas exploration and supply. Recent example is of Gas pipe from

Iran to India. These practices do boost the industrial pace. FDI flows even keep the Indian stock markets bullish and boosting market activities. Recently in 2005, India is opening more sectors for FDI, such as banking and Real Estate, coal mines and insurance and retail sectors; as well allowing higher percentage of FDI such as in telecommunication.

Market forces alone cannot determine economic future. Each country determines and draws a road map for economic reforms that would be based on its own skills, resources, strengths and vulnerabilities. To expect developing countries to continually liberalize, at an extreme pace, even within a rule based regime, may result in opposite of what is desirable.

India's labor laws deter foreign investment in some industries. It is coincidence that software and business-outsourcing companies are exempt from many labor regulations, such as those regarding hours and overtime. Without these exemptions, it would be impossible to perform back-office operations in India. To attract foreign investment in labor-intensive industries, the government should therefore consider making labor laws more flexible. Commenting on the economic survey (2005), FICCI President said. "The Survey has noted that labor laws in competing economies like China and Latin American countries are much more aligned to the requirements of a global industry than Indian laws."

Economic Survey (2005) suggests that India has remained third most attractive investment destination in Asia after China and Hong Kong. Since the FDI norms were liberalized, most of the investments have flown in for data processing, software and consultancy services, followed by pharmaceuticals and automobile industry. Power and services sectors are other big sectors that have attracted foreign investors. However on the flip side it notes that the outlook for industrial sector would be better if infrastructure bottlenecks and shortages, labor market rigidities, entry & exit barriers for firms and land acquisition and multiple stage levels of approvals-clearances are eliminated.

Some Indian policy makers might argue that the reforms

proposed here would undermine long-held social objectives, such as creating employment. But the evidence shows that regulations on foreign investment, foreign trade, and labor have actually slowed economic growth and lowered the standard of living. A decade ago, India's per capita income was nearly the same as China's; today China's is almost twice as high.

India's economy has made real progress, but further liberalization will be needed to sustain its growth. The country now has 40 million people looking for work, and an additional 35 million will join the labor force over the next three years. Creating jobs for all these Indians will require more dynamic and competitive industries across the economy.

Our second focus is the mass market for the low-end consumers in India. These mass markets are of poor, low income and rural markets. Globalization, technology, economic liberalization, and economic reforms, foreign direct investment (FDI) have facilitated it. Globalization has shown that there are low-end markets in many of the developing countries and we learnt about the different business practices in which these market needs are met.

The other above-mentioned four factors have impact also. There is more connectivity due to mobile phones and access to other technology channels and exposure to global products and services and life styles through TV etc. There is sharing of technology innovative channels since some of these like Internet have wiped out the boundaries. There is indigenous, adaptive and transfer of technology in many areas. More jobs are created which promote more consumer spend because of economic liberalization, and economic reforms, foreign direct investment (FDI). Therefore, this mass market gets further expanded. Indian businesses must communicate about the business focus to this mass market and also fine tune their business practices as communicated by mass markets demands and expectations and spend.

Our third focus is how these five factors: globalization, technology, economic liberalization, economic reforms, foreign direct investment (FDI) are applied to core competencies, people and processes in business practices.

The competencies of Indian people at all levels, has made India a global player in many businesses and has boosted the business image as well economy of India. As impact of these factors, improved business processes have facilitated production, marketing of products, services and ideas, and technology leading to further economic gains.

Major contribution of the abovementioned factors is in business communication for people (consumer) oriented change through multiple choices to work, to grow, and to consume the products and services; and changing technology and development of people's capabilities through enhanced skill as communication enablers. Technology development whether in telecommunication, transportation, infrastructure such as roads, highways, energy, water, oil etc. communicate about the business practices to deliver these to the people for their benefit. Business technology in the area of ICTs, IT, and manufacturing etc.; whether indigenous, imported or adapted have contributed to economic gains and communicated feelings of wellbeing and progress to the people.

Secondly, *communication about business practices — new or best practices to people is through business schools and other communication skills programs and through exposure to global business practices. Such business communication practices have developed better cadre of business leaders and functionaries who have even global demand. Modern trends are evident in India in new business communication practices based on yesteryears best practices. Changing trends in business education, business culture are pushing business enterprises and employees to achieve. Achievement motivation is high.*

Thirdly, *people in business work place have gained; the work place of today is better than yesterday because of technology innovations. There are improved ways of doing work. Over and above, there is concern and effort for human development as an asset to the business, better employee-management relationships and respect for the human potentiality to grow — where it fits the best. People from small towns and rural areas are being given opportunities for new communication skills training to fit in the emerging job markets. There is increased concern for their physical and psychological health. Such an approach has boosted the business productivity and therefore economic gains.*

People are always at the core of all economic activity. They gain through employment, enhanced purchasing power, better and multiple consumer choices, new products and services due to global competition and competitive prices. Due to global competition people learn, develop and upgrade both their local as well global skills. People also call for business social responsibility at global level whether to combat diseases such as HIV/AIDS, natural disasters like tsunami, or use of computer and Internet for development.

Challenge of globalization for India is to reset its economic priorities to make them people-oriented rather than commodity related. This alone will help country meet the challenges of globalization. *The people related economic policies must particularly focus on those who are worst off in society. Though raising economic growth is important, the ultimate objective should be to expand the ability of the most of sections of the society to earn a decent living.* This assumes more importance as only by providing for a certain economic security to the poorest of the poor could the country meet the challenges of the globalization. These days there is no way any economy can escape the rapid process of integrating with the world economy. Globalization is a vehicle for progress that we cannot ignore.

India is more cautious for FDI, foreign collaborations, and economic reforms. It is opening up slowly and cautiously from one focus to other. There is protectionist attitude to protect domestic companies for steady growth. They do want economic growth and employment for its people but human welfare and human relations development is also of consideration. Expats' expertise has always been utilized well — now, as well earlier. With booming economy, outsourcing models, expats are contributing expertise, funding and are in joint ventures.

India is doing efficiently and cautiously both — *opening*

up businesses for outsourcing, economic liberalization and FDI; *and opening the society*. These two can develop in parallel. *That is how India envisions its problem and development — emerging and surging.*

In business practices, India does not strive to match with China. It may have healthy competition with it. Both differ because their focuses for business development and practices have altogether different perspectives though they may follow the basic models. But its connotations are different for the two countries. China can learn marketing and management expertise, and business culture adaptation from India. India's business enterprises can learn aggressive business capturing from China. Its workers can learn the value of hard work and diligence, efficiency and business discipline from within. Both are major contributing factors for any business success.

Chinese model of business practices may be good to follow for business success but it cannot overlook the good practices for the development of people in businesses that boost productivity. If employees, people are provided well, given challenging opportunity why would they like to migrate to distant lands, leaving behind the culture, the people they love, and the ties that bond them? They can do more for the country's businesses as expats are doing — providing the expertise in good business practices adapted from other countries. This applies to both India and China.

In India, domestic companies with different marketing strategies are handling its low-end mass markets. The consumer spend in this market is additionally contributing to the domestic capabilities of the companies and creating more revenues for them. China has yet to tap this big and rapid growing market.

In terms of population, China and India are home to the largest number of the poorest people in the world. Here there are two main ways in which MNEs (multinational enterprises) are helping to alleviate poverty. The first is by investing in the relatively prosperous industrializing areas; in doing so they provide more jobs and raise the income levels of people in these areas. These benefits are now spreading to other parts of these two large countries where, in 10 years or so, abject poverty is most likely to be cut back. The second is by investment in vital physical infrastructure in the heartland of China and India; this is most often undertaken jointly with indigenous firms and supported by aid agencies and the host governments. It is a necessary preparatory step to further investment by MNEs.

Our above observations are also pointer to the fact that models of globalization, globalism and glocalization; the three factors of economic reforms and liberalization and foreign direct investments and the outsourcing models; when applied to the core competencies, people and processes; have different outcomes for both India and China. Both are emerging markets, focusing on economic gains and being powerful economically. But they are likely to grow in these two directions differently because the characteristics of its people differ, the aspirations as well economic policies, Political leadership and Political Will for its people differ. The market forces will mold the business practices differently for these two countries. As such China and India are taking different paths to economic prosperity as per their business strengths.

In short, Business Communication is important in the above scenarios at various levels. Globalization suggests communication with international businesses through exposure to business styles, practices, products and services of these businesses. Such exposure is through media channels, interpersonal channels and travels and other supporting technologies. Such information and knowledge expand new businesses, innovate others, and create new demands for products and services and promote global partnerships. The two premise of Intercultural Communication: cultural sensitivity, specifically of business culture, and intercultural communication competence is important in these contexts. This is equally important for globalism for having local impact and for global model since local talents, local products, public and other business practices would be used.

Public relation as a communicative medium is important to create visibility, credibility, and image building of businesses and their products and services among global partners, foreign countries and their governments, and international media. PR promotes businesses, partnerships and foreign direct investments. We cannot underplay the role of fast growing Information Communication Technologies — both hardware and software that create instant connectivity, global availability and accessibility of business innovations and business solutions.

It is an observation that *different emerging markets have their business strengths and weaknesses according to their specific models of business communication practices.* Some of these are emerging as booming markets as interplay of abovementioned three factors and other additional models but their *markets develop according to models of their predominant business strengths.*

There are Visionaries – the Business Legends; who have brought India to the world and who are the true driving force behind the great Indian success story. They are living legends, the people who have built India's corporate fortune. They are indeed the foundation, the basis, of the great economic strides that India has been making in the last few decades.

India's aspiration to be the dominant player in the global arena presents a rosy picture of its society and capabilities. But on the other hand, it does face the limitations and helplessness in dealing with poverty and the problems of absolute poverty. This presents dismal picture of Indian society and its people.

With the aspiration to be the dominant player in the global arena and problem of absolute poverty, with such rosy and the dismal picture running parallel; India is forging ahead to create a strong economy within the framework of globalization, globalism and glocalization; and through the visions of its governance, business legends, and its people.

References

Albrow M. and King E.: *Globalization, Knowledge, and Society*. Sage Publications, London, 1990.

Amadco Lodovico: *India from Emerging to Surging*, Mackinsey Quarterly.com, 2001.

Dutton William H. (ed.): *Information and Communication Technologies: Visions and Realities*. Oxford University Press, New York, 1996.

Diana Farrell & Adil Zainulbhai: *Richer Future for India*, Mackinsey Quarterly.com, 2004.

Diana Farrell et al.: Beyond Cheap Labor, *Developing Economies*, Mackinsey Quarterly.com, 2005.

Dixon Patrick *Futurewise: Six Faces of Global Change*, Profile Books, 2003.

Derek H. Chen and Carl J. Dahlman: *Knowledge and Development: A Cross Section Approach*, World Bank Paper, 2003.

Dunning John H. (ed.): *Regions, Globalization and the Knowledge Based Economy*, Oxford University Press, 2002.

Edge David: The Social Shaping of Technology, Heap Nick, Ray Thomas et al. (eds.) *Information Technology and Society*, Sage Publications, London, 1995.

Economic Survey of Apex Economic Associations India (2005).

Gore A.: Basic Principles in Building Information Society, *Global Issues on Line Serial,* Sept. 1996.

Hanson J. and Narula Uma: *New Communication Technologies in Developing Countries*, New Jersey, Lawrence Erlbaum Associates, 1990.

Narula Uma: The Cultural Challenge of Communication Technology. *American Behavioural Scientist.* Vol. 32, No. 2, Nov-Dec. 1988, pp. 194-207, Sage Publications, Newburyport, USA.

Narula Uma: *Communication Perspectives: Cultural Diffusion, Dynamics and Challenges,* HarAnand Publications, New Delhi, 2000.

Narula Uma: *Mass Media Communication Technologies: New Perspectives,* HarAnand Publications, New Delhi, 2001.

Narula Uma: *Let Us Do It Ourselves* mimeo World Bank, 2000.

Narula Uma: *Technology Revisited: India Case Study* mimeo 2003.

Narula Uma: *International Communication: Discourses* mimeo 2003.

Narula Uma: *Diffusion of Cell Phone in India and Social Change,* Research Publication 2005.

Narula Uma: *Business Practices: Modern Trends,* Atlantic Publishers & Distributors (P) Ltd., New Delhi, 2006.

Narula Uma: *Handbook of Communication Models, Perspectives, Strategies,* Atlantic Publishers & Distributors (P) Ltd., New Delhi, 2006.

Narula Uma: *Dynamics of Mass Communications,* Atlantic Publishers & Distributors (P) Ltd., New Delhi, 2006.

Narula Uma: *Communication Models,* Atlantic Publishers & Distributors (P) Ltd., New Delhi, 2006.

Prahalad C.K. & Venkat Ramaswamy (a): *The Future of Competition: Co-creating Unique Values with Customers.* Harvard Business School Press, 2004.

Prahalad C.K. & Stuart Hart (b): *The Fortunes at the Bottom of the Pyramid 2004.*

Prahalad C.K. (c): *Interview with Hindustan Times*, New Delhi, Aug. 18, 2004.

Prahalad C.K. (d): The Invisible Market, *Across the Board*, Sept./Oct., 2004.

Prahalad C.K. and Al Hammond: Serving the World's Poor, Profitably, *Harvard Business Review*, 2004.

Appendix

Economics of Basic Minimum Needs

There is impact of corrupt practices, ineffective rules and regulations on people's basic minimum needs of shelter, safe drinking water, food, sanitation, vis-à-vis growth and prosperity of people in India. These practices play upon the economics of health, education, diversity and infrastructure and overall Welfare Model for people.

The varied inefficient and corrupt practices of politicians, bureaucracy, people and businesses can undermine and have negative impact on the economic growth and prosperity of people. These are everyday practices in our daily lives; but important part and parcel of our existence. The impact on people's basic minimum needs such as housing affordability, safe drinking water, sanitation, judiciary effectiveness, infrastructure, and economics of health is critical. Housing affordability is a critical aspect of economic growth, and the quest for human community starts by ending housing policies that result in children being raised in squalor, deprivation, danger, and disease. Equally important is safe drinking water, sanitation, garbage disposal, unadulterated food, clean environment for economics of health. Economics of education, employment and welfare model for people is absolute necessary for prosperity.

Housing affordability, corruption: The politician and bureaucracy is weak role model to the public such as in not evicting the official residential accommodation when they are no longer in office. When they do not even pay the utilities charges of electricity, water, and telephone etc. for years and which may run into several Crore. The common person cannot get his own house legitimately vacated through honoring of rent/lease contracts or even through the courts for number of years. He uses corrupt ways (thus corruption is legitimized) to get it vacated for his genuine needs. Even underworld penetrates in these transactions, when Government spends more on law and order controls properties worth millions are transacted this way. Take a recent example of a swindler, who swindled people of millions worth property through political and police connections with his simple strategy of getting into disputed property deals where law of the land was not helping them. Secondly, people are not either building residential and commercial properties or they keep them locked for fear of not getting them vacated when needed. Thus residential properties are not in circulation, there is acute shortage of houses and even rentals go up because of low supply.

The net economic effect is that people cannot afford adequate shelters and that affects their quality of life.

Further, these cases have much deeper implications for the Indian State than its obvious political overtones. Money blocked in locked properties does not circulate in the market. This anomaly happens when laws and rules of the land are not even respected by the lawmakers.

Moreover, Judiciary is ineffective and overburdened with numerous court cases pending for years and years and financially burdening the small and big litigants.

Litigants cannot expect justice in their lifetime. This further depresses the economic scene.

By not making utility payments running into Crore, the government and public economies suffer. Payments made could have been spent in improving the utilities such as electricity, water, telephone etc. Either by vacating on own, or even through the court orders, they would have shown respect for the effectiveness of rules, regulations and laws of the country.

The greedy politicians and toeing bureaucrats make rules ineffective. First they spent public money, time and efforts in setting guidelines for executing various activities; then they themselves do not follow those guidelines. They lower the status of judiciary by not respecting the 'justices' in operation with all their experience and wisdom. *This is setting wrong role model for the public. The root cause is corruption for personal gains but it affects the overall economy.*

The issue of housing affordability is both an economic growth issue for the business community, and a serious moral crisis for those of us concerned about families and the destructive division of society into rich and poor.

We must house our citizens decently. The skyrocketing rents create more division between the rich and poor. For low-income renters – it is crisis. It is not just personal crisis but should be taken as community crisis. Fundamentally, the income of average working people is not keeping pace with the cost of living, and housing supply is not keeping up with the demand. A large percentage of people live in 'shelter poverty' i.e. they pay so much on rents that they cannot afford basic necessities of life.

The issue is of overcoming the vast array of obstacles and impediments that prevent the adequate production of affordable rental and ownership houses. Housing affordability is a critical aspect of economic growth, and the quest for human community starts by ending housing policies that result in children being raised in squalor, deprivation, danger, and disease. The motto should be a decent home in a decent community for every family.

Economics of Health involves safe drinking water and sanitation, garbage disposal, and wholesome food and medical aid.

Unsafe drinking water: *People are suffering. There is scarcity of water for human consumption. People are suffering and dying of gastroenteritis since they are drinking unsafe water. There is no alternative but to drink un-potable water.*

This is even happening in the capital of India – Delhi;

though small towns' water safety is ignored and the villages are worst sufferers. Ground water is polluted in Delhi. The pollution level at local river Yumna is 70%; not even fit for bathing; and imagine its water is the source for drinking water for majority of Delhi population. Invariably the underground drinking water supply and sewage lines get mixed at some point and water gets polluted. There is very low checks and accountability for this kind of incidents. The pesticide, heavy metal and hazardous material are in the water and government does not have facilities to treat it. The water pipes are old and eroded and are releasing the lead in the water. These are some of the pollutants in the water beside the small scale industries who were discharging their effluents in the river. The tube wells are not safe water source because of ground water pollution.

Situation in rural areas is still worse. A large number of the villages in India still do not have safe drinking water supply. There is no tap water supply. The source for drinking water supply is traditional wells, tube-wells and hand pumps. Many times water content lacks fluoride. With the result, teeth fall prematurely of villagers who drink this kind of water; and lead in water age them prematurely. Government has been making efforts to some extent but it is a stupendous task that calls for more efforts and money and urgency. There is scarcity of unsafe drinking water both in rural and urban areas. Delhi tops the list.

A study of Indira Gandhi Institute for Development Research (IGIDR) Mumbai points that the World Bank has estimated that more than 30 million life years are wasted annually due to water related diseases. This amounts to an annual loss of Rs. 36,000 Crore valued at per capita income of Rs 12,000. In a sense this is what we would have spent for clean water and sanitation. Given its importance for human welfare, this sector requires a goal-oriented strategy and a target date for 100% coverage. Sewage treatment plants of adequate capacities should be mandatory for every town.

Economics of unsafe drinking water are enormous. Count the money spent on treating the health hazards! The money spent on checking or not checking (the supervisors can ignore their duty) the water system. The corruption involved in not changing the old pipes; though government might have sanctioned money for it. The industries despite of Supreme Court order still throw pollutants in the Yumna River and more and more money is spent on litigation. Further, it is ironic, government spends money on information and education campaigns for safe drinking water. The responsible attitude of workers, industrialists, government, and citizens can definitely deliver safe drinking water and better health and its economics will be better.

Garbage disposal and sanitation: The garbage litters in commercial and residential complexes creating all kinds of health hazards. It is citizens' duty to dispose it but equally important is that government takes responsibility to manage disposal of the garbage through providing dustbins, trucks to pick the garbage, disposal sites both area wise and central dumpsites and later recycling and incinerating of the garbage. The local governments ignore all the responsibilities to the extent that High Court has to direct Delhi local government to choose site for garbage disposal. So far garbage management has not assumed importance in full for government or private sectors though it needs urgent attention.

Less cleanliness is maintained in eating places. A restaurant or an eating place on the roadside may be clean inside and serving good food; but the piles of rubbish outside can be a source of infection. Or the practice of just rinsing the used tea-cups in a bucket of water can cause enough infection for gastroenteritis.

There is scarcity of water everywhere both in urban and rural areas. People understand the necessity of washing hands after toilet. But when there is no water in public toilets, hand washing is ignored. Imagine unwashed hands of the restaurants' employees or other workers and thus creating problems of E-coli bacteria all the time. Public toilets also stink as there is no water to flush the solid waste.

Unsafe drinking water or even bathing in that water is health hazard. But there is scarcity of running water also. It is scarcer in bigger and overpopulated cities. How does one live, survive without water or limited water? With the result there is no proper maintenance of public toilets, sanitation, sewage, and public buildings. Lack of proper cleanliness can be bigger hazard than all the medical facilities put together.

The slums in Delhi are overpopulated, dirty, no electricity, and unsafe water through hand pumps only, or tap water in the houses. There are open drains and no proper sewage. The polluted environment and dismal living conditions exist close to the clean and elite residential areas without any qualms. Two strands of life co-exist. (take example of slum close to IIT Delhi and construction sites close by). Why cannot government/ builders spend on Sulabh Shuchalya for toilets which are inexpensive and create cleaner sanitation?

Imagine the environment pollution due to poor or no sanitation, poor garbage disposal, industrial pollution, hospital waste pollution and even the problem of pollution created by polythene bags for packaging and carrying goods when not disposed properly. Such pollution is hazardous to health and living conditions. Government, Industry and people have to assume positive role to combat environment pollution.

Food adulteration: All kinds of adulterated food are sold in the market. Cereals, spices, cooking oil, and even milk are adulterated with poisonous chemicals. People would like to trust at least government dairy plants. But it goes unchecked many times. People drink adulterated milk all the time. They buy expensive milk but suffer from health hazards and nutrition loss. Cooking mustard oil is adulterated with poisonous chemicals; people consuming it die of Dropsy disease. The spices of daily use such as turmeric, salt and chilies etc. are mixed with hazardous substances; thus creating more health hazards then the beneficial effects of these spices. Even fruits and vegetables are not spared; the chemicals are injected to make it sweeter in taste or look brighter in color. The motive is to make extra money.

People keep buying some of these absolutely necessary products. Dropsy deaths as short-term consequence and health hazards as long term consequences continue. *Government continues spending on curative health care and also on setting up the Food Inspectorate to check adulteration.* But food adulteration continues on large scale, traders do not care about any warnings, crack teams are not able to take action. The root cause is corruption.

Food adulteration happens all the time and is very frequent because of inefficient system of checking adulteration. On one hand, the labs across the country are not well equipped to check adulterations of many kinds. On the other hand, the corrupt practices of government food inspectors, such as not checking the food samples regularly in general and in particular cases; and taking bribes from food manufacturers when they know food is adulterated; adds on to the inefficient system.

These instances reveal that root cause is corruption, both in government system and among people. People's health suffers because of their own doing; and through the government's lackadaisical attitude towards checking adulteration and public health issues. The inter-link is that people tend to be corrupt as they want to make fast buck and the inefficiency of government system encourages them. Thus people themselves as well government have low concerns for public health.

The impact of these situations is on public health and management of economy. The significance is that public health suffers because of corrupt and inefficient practices. In the long run government has to spend more money on treating the public health issues. The media campaigns to create awareness about nutrition value of food are a waste. The critical impact is on not able to improve the quality of life for masses.

Again our economics are not good. Money spent on maintenance of residential and commercial complexes go waste. Money spent on creating the infrastructure of garbage disposal is wasted since government does spend but with no accountability for the delivery of services. Money spent on checking adulteration and efforts to provide healthy food is wasted; and so is money spent on awareness campaigns for healthy food. Rather further health problems are created which need more money.

All that is needed are the accountability, responsibility, and efficiency of government and people equally.

Economics of Welfare Model: Absolute poverty problem has created beggary in the country. It is higher in the urban areas. It is both political and social issue. It is a political issue because absolute poor and the poor are not adequately placed in the 'Welfare Model' of India. Socially, we do not like people to beg. Able bodied beggars may be willing to work. Government does not provide any skill training to them or job opportunities. Public may not trust them to give work. When they have no work, no purchasing power, they beg for food and clothing. They go hungry or get fed and clothed depending on people's charity. Rain, sunshine or cold, they live by the road side. They use roads for civic amenities. The result, you have urine and feces stench around you.

Solicitation at every corner of the road, and even in your houses at all times of the day intrude on your privacy and irritates you. At times it can even create law and order situation also. But majority of them are so low at the economic ladder, they do not know what to do. It is a sheer waste of human potentialities when you see an able bodied man soliciting to sell a magazine or a packet of incense at the traffic light intersections. Or beggars would knock on the car windows, children showing a broken leg or a missing hand. You feel compassion and helpless. Your few rupees (cents) will not even buy him food; and how many you can help. It is a problem to be solved at the root.

Government welfare model practically has nothing for them. As public policy, government provides free education to all through government schools; and medical aid to all through government hospitals and dispensaries. *But who will let a beggar child attend a school or get medical aid in the government hospital since they are treated as social outcasts.* Poverty further perpetuates poverty as they beget children!

Children attending government schools lose interest and drop out. The reason being most of the lower social class children attend these schools. Teachers are highly trained, highly paid, and comes from higher social class. They are not motivated to teach these children for two reasons. One is the assumption that these children are not brainy, ambitious, and achievement-oriented — this being the usual stereotype for children of lower social classes. This is an impediment for these children to benefit from the huge amount of government spend and efforts.

The significance is that there is no reality check on economics of low wage earners. The negligible social insurance for low wage earners in unorganized sector (for them and their dependent families) further pushes them to poverty and also to corrupt and crime practices. Government must ensure basic facilities and work for people, otherwise not only they will suffer in poverty but will also become criminals and militants. Crime and terrorism will increase which will consume more of government funds than providing the basic facilities to them.

The economics of good living through education and employment thus goes haywire by biases for lower social class. Government has to organize the absolute poor, create work opportunities for them, empower them enough to meet the basic necessities of life of food, shelter, clothing, education, medical aid etc. through welfare programs of cash and kind.

Economics of Manpower: India has huge manpower. Is all the manpower utilized? The unemployment rate in the country can fall if we focus on three pronged strategy: i) assessment of manpower needs for the next 5 to 10 years through manpower forecasts; ii) creating skilled manpower accordingly through educational and training programs with changed manpower demands; and iii) match the skills with jobs. How much economic wastage occurs when jobs are created because there is urgent need, they are not filled due to sheer lack of inertia and insights; and people devoid of opportunity for the jobs live a life of want and its consequences for the family and society.

As we have observed in the recent past, and has also

realized currently that opportunities and businesses created by globalization, such as Outsourcing and varied Technology businesses are demanding more educated and skilled manpower to fit in. If we in India rise to the occasion, there is no doubt the employment rate goes up, economic growth happens and people are economically prosperous and socially contented and a resource.

Economics of Infrastructure: Development of infrastructure is crucial for sustainable economic growth. India can push up its growth figures by developing its infrastructure. The deficiencies in infrastructure have been major drag on economic development and development in general. The crisis faced now is a compounded result of long neglect of the urgent needs for capacity augmentation and productivity improvement. Roads, ports, railways and Highways are particularly stretched beyond their capacity limits. Their performance and service quality are below international norms. Power shortage is acute and new power grids for electric supply are needed both for industrial and commercial development and human consumption for basic quality of life.

The old paradigm of public monopoly for providing basic infrastructure is no longer valid in the light of *rapidly expanding demand for quality infrastructure for businesses and resulting economic growth in globalization contexts*. Credible and transparent systems for attracting large scale private investment; the professional management of infrastructure by commercial entities; and full accountability by them should be the norm. Privatization can have five modes such as corporatization, contract operation and management, long-term concessions such as BOT (build-operate-transfer), divestiture with regulation, and divestiture with deregulation.

Economics of Diversity: Social class, caste barriers, regional barriers and even language barriers create identity crisis in India; both socially and politically. These create more development, political and economic dilemmas and are hurdles for economic prosperity of large number of people as divisive inequalities get built through these dimensions.

Subject Index

W